A Pocket Guide to
Environmental
Bad Guys

James Ridgeway
and
Jeffrey St. Clair

Thunder's Mouth Press
New York

Research Note: Sales figures are for 1997 unless otherwise noted; political contributions and lobby fees come from Center for Responsive Politics; CEO salaries are from filings with Securities and Exchange Commission or Paywatch web site. Other data from Hoovers, *Fortune*, and Securities and Exchange Commission.

Published by
Thunder's Mouth Press
841 Broadway, 4th Floor
New York, NY 10003

First Edition
First printing, 1998

Library of Congress
Cataloging-in-Publication Data

Ridgeway, James, 1936-
    Environmental bad guys / James Ridgeway
and Jeffrey St. Clair.
        p.   cm.
    ISBN 1-56025-153-0
    1. Environmental management. 2. Environmen-talists 3. Environmentalism. 4. Nature—Effect of human beings on. I. St. Clair, Jeffrey. II. Title.
GE300.R53 1999
363.7'02'0973—c21   98-34022
                                                            CIP

Cover design by Great American Art Company
Book design by Ed Hedemann
Printed in the United States of America

The rancher (with a few honorable exceptions) is a man who strings barbed wire all over the range; drills wells and bulldozes stock ponds; drives off elk and antelope and bighorn sheep; poisons coyotes and prairie dogs; shoots eagles, bears, and cougars on sight; supplants the native grasses with tumbleweed, snakeweed, povertyweed, cowshit, anthills, mud, dust, and flies. And then leans back and grins at the TV cameras and talks about how he loves the American West.

Edward Abbey

Contents

Introduction

The American environmental movement traces its ideological roots back to two often competing sources in the late nineteenth century, the utilitarian conservationists led by Teddy Roosevelt and his friend Gifford Pinchot, and the preservationists led by Sierra Club founder John Muir and Robert Marshall, the early champion of wilderness and the rights of Native Americans.

Roosevelt and his supporters preached conservation of natural resources as part of a broad doctrine of efficiency aimed at making the wisest use of natural resources. Rather than continue with rapacious capitalism in which ranchers and small farmers fought one another across the plains, Roosevelt sought efficiency through combination of businesses.

For most of this century the conservationists, who promoted regulated exploitation of the environment, have held sway. Under this regime, a dense thicket of environmental laws has been cultivated and a huge environmental bureaucracy has evolved to administrate these laws and regulations. The great era of conservationists culminated during the Nixon era with the creation of the Environmental Protection Agency, Occupational Safety and Health Administration, and the Council on Environmental Quality and the passage of the landmark laws and regulations such as the Clean Water Act, National Environmental Policy Act, and Endangered Species Act. Today nearly every agency of the federal government has an environmental office, including the FBI and the CIA.

By the 1980s, however, it was becoming clear to many that this plethora of agencies were on the verge of being captured by the very industries and businesses they were supposed to regulate. The evidence for this was written on the landscape. Despite well intentioned laws and regulations, air pollution in many areas of the country was worsening, cancer rates were climbing, record numbers of animals and plants were being added to the endangered species list, and ancient forests on public lands were falling at a rate faster than the rain forests of the Amazon. The reasons for this are undeniably complex. But a major factor has been the industry's ability to manipulate the system. Inside the Beltway, the pollution lobby out spends the green lobby by a more than 10 to 1 margin. Oil and chemical lobbyists have actually had a hand in writing many of the recent laws and regulations governing toxic waste and air pollution.

This predicament has prompted the reemergence of a more radical and grass-roots based environmental movement, one that tends to advocate homegrown solutions that are permanent, self-regulating, and not subject to political manipulation. Perhaps the most potent example of this trend is the growing Zero Cut movement, a grassroots crusade to end commercial logging on the national forests, the old symbol of Pinchot's utilitarian vision.

This book sets forth an outline of the power structure arrayed against the environment, including companies, organizations, and individuals. The authors hope it will be an organizing tool, both in terms of opening up a new perspective in thinking about the subject, and as a help to grassroots activists.

September 1998

ACKNOWLEDGMENTS

I am grateful to the Schumann Foundation for its support of my research into the environment. This research underlies much of this book. Special thanks to Gaelle Drevet, who helped with research and reporting. For information on the effects of chlorine I am indebted to the work of Eric Coppolino and his fine article in *Sierra Magazine*. Thanks to Alliance for Nuclear Accountability, American Public Power Association, Project Underground, Ann Leonard, Kenny Bruno, Alex Beauchamps, Brian Lipsett on the waste trade, Sheila Kaplan for reporting on lobbying, Critical Mass, Greenpeace, Marcia Carroll, Center for Health, Environment & Justice, Winona Houter, Jim Riccio, Rick Hind, Charlie Cray, Mineral Policy Center, Center for Responsive Politics, Environmental Working Group, Environmental Advocates (Albany, NY), Environmental Background Information Center, Clare Saliba, Gene Coyle, Ed Hedemann did the excellent design and edited the manuscript. Thanks also to Daniel O'Connor and Neil Ortenberg at Thunder's Mouth Press, and to my agent Faith Childs.

James Ridgeway

Larry Tuttle, director of the Center for Environmental Equity, is owed a huge thanks for information on mining and grazing policy. But equally important, Tuttle gave us fresh insight into intricate politics of the environmental movement. Steve Kelly, politician, painter and environmental activist, imparted crucial information on trout, wilderness, and forest policy. Kelly's comrade, Mike Bader, who runs the Alliance for the Wild Rockies, was also an invaluable source on everything from grizzly bears to the management of Yellowstone Park. Tim Hermach, Michael Donnelly, and Carl Ross gave a wealth of statistics on forests. Randal O'Toole, president of the Thoreau Institute, is one of the best environmental economists in the business and he shared his unique knowledge of how the federal budget influences the behavior of the Forest Service and the Bureau of Land Management. Patty Clary, who runs Californians Against Toxins, never failed to return a call when we needed to know one more picky detail about an obscure but lethal chemical. Patty is fearless and without peer. No one knows more about public lands grazing than Susan Schock, founder of Gila Watch, and she patiently taught us the ins-and-outs of this complex and contentious subject. Winona Howder at Critical/Mass Energy Project was a key source on nuclear energy and utility deregulation. Bob Kuehn and his students at the embattled Tulane Environmental Law Clinic were generous with their knowledge of environmental justice law, Louisiana politics and the history of the Shintech plant slated for Convent. Michael Colby and Jennifer Ferrera of Food and Water provided reams of data on meat companies, food irradiation and bovine growth hormones. Bernardo Issel helped gather information for the profiles of the big environmental groups. Danny Kennedy and his colleagues at Project Underground provided invaluable information on oil and mining companies. The Handleman Foundation and the Levinson Foundation are owed a special debt of gratitude for their financial support. Several of the topics in this book were originally reported on by St. Clair and Alex Cockburn in our column "Nature and Politics." No thanks, of course, can repay Kimberly Willson-St. Clair for her advice, encouragement, and endurance.

Jeffrey St. Clair

P A R T 1

Resource-Depleters

Energy

EVER SINCE THE ARAB OIL embargo of the late 1970s, the big international energy corporations have raced to control the last of the world's fossil fuel energy resources, focusing on the vast untapped resources of the far north. They are seeking to secure leases on every mile of the United States's Alaskan coast in the Arctic against the time when the U.S.'s own extensive store of energy resources becomes too expensive to extract.

THE THREAT OF GLUT

And there is another reason. While political debate often focuses on the eventual exhaustion of resources and the pollution caused by their burning, the main problem *for the industry* has always been the threat of glut. It is for that reason that the industry has entered into an extraordinary system of alli-

"We're from the power company. We're here to help."

ances and cartels around the world to prevent reckless competition from burying it alive. A century ago, Rockefeller's Standard Oil gained control of the "black tide" flooding out of western Pennsylvania through a complex network of kickbacks and rebates on the railroads. Through two world wars a handful of western companies built an international cartel that carved up Middle Eastern oil. The creation of Organization of Petroleum Exporting Countries (Saudi Arabia, etc.) during the energy crisis never seriously challenged that western-controlled network.

Energy and environmental policy in Congress are not set by any sort of determined debate of an elected legislature, but by groups of special interests which write and submit the bills. When it comes to energy, for example, regional interests—representing business—can set far-reaching national policy.

When it comes to energy, regional interests set national policy.

That was the case in 1995 when the Louisiana and Alaskan congressional delegations joined in attempting to promote the interests of the energy industry. Senator Bennett Johnston of oil-rich Louisiana joined with Sen. Ted Stevens of oil-rich Alaska to promote drilling in the National Arctic Wildlife Refuge. In addition, the two groups of legislators succeeded for the first time in pushing through legislation that would allow Alaskan oil to be exported to foreign markets, mainly China and Japan.

Continued Growth Anticipated

As the century ends, the industry anticipates continued growth, due in large part to the auto industry's successful marketing of the gas-guzzling sport utility vehicles, which is credited with the long-term surge in gas consumption, all but obliterating savings the government had sought to achieve by setting fuel efficiency standards. A few years ago the industry fought regulation of natural gas on grounds

How much would you contribute for a socialistic U.S.A.?

A private power company ad placed in magazines during the 1950s.

the nation was fast running out of supplies. Now there is so much gas that it is becoming a fuel of choice for power generation plants to replace pollution-causing coal. Coal in turn is finding new markets in the developing world where pollution standards are reduced. In the U.S. increased coal min-

ing is projected to occur in the strip mines of the
West.

FIGHTING GOVERNMENT REGULATION

One of the most important weapons in fighting
off glut and unchecked competition has been government regulation, employed by the companies to
organize their markets. Federal regulation preempts
conflicting rules imposed by various states, and because the oil industry historically has been able to
exercise such influence
with Congress, it has
been able to use the tool
of regulation to control
the production of oil in
its own interests. Cur-
rently the industry is
engaged in a vigorous campaign to reorganize the
electric utility industry—heretofore subject to a
modicum of independent and local governmental
control.

Electric utilities are responsible
for two-thirds of sulfur dioxide
emissions, one-third of nitrogen
dioxide emissions, and much of
the nuclear waste.

The production of energy, especially electricity,
is the root cause of much of our pollution and the
driving force behind global warming trends. Electric utilities are responsible for two-thirds of sulfur
dioxide emissions, one-third of nitrogen dioxide
emissions, and substantial amounts of nuclear waste
in the U.S.

Electric utilities represent the one branch of the
energy industry that has been regulated. And despite
shortcomings, it is often cited as a major factor in
blocking an energy monopoly that would include
electricity, something that the old holding companies at the turn of the century craved.

Dark Days at Black Mesa

Black Mesa, a hundred-square-mile seam of low-sulfur coal that is the richest deposit in North America, lies on disputed ground, claimed by both the Navajo and Hopi tribes. But there's little dispute over who owns the coal. Through a series of shady deals, it ended up in the hands of Peabody Coal, owned by the English conglomerate Hanson, PLC. Peabody operates two large mining sites on the reservation, the Kayenta mine and the Black Mesa mine. Seven million tons of coal are gouged out of the Kayenta deposit each year. The coal is hauled by an electric railroad to a coal-fired generating plant at Page, Arizona, overlooking Glen Canyon. The Black Mesa mine yields five million tons of coal a year which is sluiced through a 300-mile pipeline in a slurry mix of coal and water. The water is drawn from the now rapidly shrinking Navajo aquifer and more than 50 springs in this desert area have vanished. Peabody dismisses concerns of water depletion by remarking that the 1.3 billion gallons of water pumped out a year is a "teaspoon from a bucket."

> Navajo and Hopi lands ravaged by Peabody Coal.

The degradation of the area is not merely a matter of aquifer depletion. Over the past 15 years there have been numerous poisonings and die-offs among Navajo livestock drinking water from springs and wells near the mines. Tests show that the water had been contaminated with high levels of lead, arsenic, and copper. The company has also been cited for illegal dumping and for leaky underground storage tanks. The constant shroud of coal dust on the mesa has proven a health hazard for livestock and people. One of the big problems has been the effects of blasting, with the shock waves leveling Navajo hogans.

When Peabody won its coal leases, the company was given an exemption from the Antiquities Act, allowing it to mine on burial grounds. The only proviso is that a medicine man should be brought in to perform a perfunctory ceremony in the general area of the land to be excavated. In 1993, a particularly horrifying year for the Navajo, no less than four burial grounds were mined. "The remains of our ancestors are being dug up and shipped to the place where they burn the coal," says Louise Benally of the Navaho Nation.

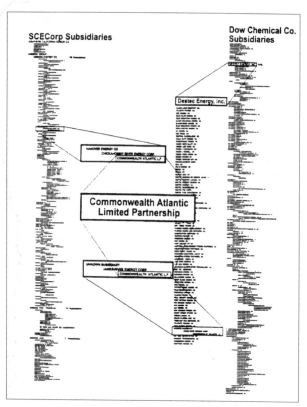

SCECorp Subsidiaries

Dow Chemical Co.
Subsidiaries

Destec Energy, Inc.

Commonwealth Atlantic
Limited Partnership

This extraordinarily complex interlock diagram,
constructed by the American Public Power Association,
illustrates the relationship among the electric utility
Commonweath Atlantic, Dow Chemical, other
companies, and their subsidiaries.

In Washington, as well as on Wall Street, utility
deregulation is promoted as the harbinger of free-
market competition that will bring better service at
cheaper prices. To that end, it is being sold to the
public the same way airline, trucking, rail, and phone

deregulation have been sold over the past two decades. In their fantasy future world, deregulation proponents see hated monstrosities, like New York's Consolidated Edison or California's PG&E, being transformed into smaller, competitive companies.

Proposed insert
to go with electric bills
after deregulation:

E L E C T R I C I T Y   F A C T S
ABC Company

Generation Price	Average Use per Month	250 kWh	500 kWh	1000 kWh	2000kWh
Average price per kWh at different levels of use. Prices do not include regulated charges for customer services and delivery.	Average Price per kWh	4.5 cents	4.5 cents	4.5 cents	5 cents

Your average generation price will vary according to when and how much electrkity you consume. See your most recent bill for your monthly use and your Terms of Service for the actual prices.

Contract	**Minimum Length:** 3 Years (30-day notice required for termination. Penalties may apply)	**Contact Terms:** Fixed price over contract period.

Power Sources
Demand for this electricty in the preceding 12 months was assigned generation from the following sources.

Power Sources	%	Power Sources	%
Biomass	8	Coal	10
Hydro: Large	16	Hydro: Small	2
Imported power	5	Municipal Trash	15
Natural Gas	5	Nuclear	4
Oil	24	Other Renewable	4
Solar	5	Wind	2

Air Emissions
Carbon dioxide (CO_2), Nitrogen Oxide (NO_2), and sulfur dioxide (SO_2) emissions rates from these sources, relative to the regional average.

Regional Average

CO_2
NO_2
SO_2

Lower Emissions   Higher Emissions

Notes
1 Electricity customers in New England are served by an integrated power grid, not particular generating units. The above information is on all generating units assigned to this electricity product. To obtain information on all generating units owned by, or under contract to, ABC Company, call 1-800-123-4567.
2 See reverse side and your contract terms and conditions for further information on this label. You may also call ABC Company at 1-800-123-4567, or the AAAAA Utility Commission at 1-800-987-6543.

Shell's Corporate Propaganda
Reaction to Protests Regarding Shell's Operations
in the Indigenous Lands of Nigeria and Peru

Shell Oil Company

One Shell Plaza
P.O. Box 2463
Houston, Texas 77252-2463

Dear ████

This will acknowledge receipt of your recent post card addressed to Mr. Carroll
regarding Nigeria and Peru. He has asked me to respond.

First, we must point out that Shell Oil Company, a U.S. corporation, has no operations
in either Nigeria or Peru, nor does it set policy for or control the Royal Dutch/Shell-
owned companies operating in those countries.

Attempts to link Nigeria and Peru are misleading and disingenuous. Additionally, many
of the reports received here in the U.S. regarding various events and activities in each
of these countries are distorted, misleading or erroneous.

Shell Prospecting and Development B.V., Peru (SPDP), the Royal Dutch/Shell group
company evaluating the potential for natural gas production in Peru, has publicly
committed to undertaking any operations in Peru in a manner which is open,
transparent, fully consultative and a model for future activities. It has committed to
respecting the rights and protecting the health of the indigenous people and to setting
the highest environmental standards for operation.

The situation in Nigeria is entirely different. It is one that has evolved over the past
fifty years. Social, cultural, political and economic issues facing Nigeria are complex
and intertwined. To expect the Shell Petroleum Development Company of Nigeria
(SPDC) to resolve these issues is unrealistic. Nevertheless, SPDC believes that it is
a positive presence in Nigeria.

We are forwarding your comments to Shell International Petroleum Company in
London which deals directly with the Royal Dutch/Shell Group companies operating
in Nigeria and Peru. They will communicate directly with you.

Thank you for writing us.

Sincerely,

W. K. Jacobs
W. K. Jacobs
Manager, External Affairs
Corporate & CEO Support

A Response to Shell

Critics Respond to Shell's Propaganda

Shell-Peru, Shell-Nigeria and Shell Oil (USA) are all members of the Royal Dutch Shell Group of Companies. No one has claimed that Shell Oil controls the Group — only that they have influence and input into policies. If transnational corporations such as Shell are to be held fully accountable, their actions must be judged on a global scale.

The same parent, Royal Dutch Shell, owns Shell-Nigeria and Shell-Peru, and policies for the Group affect operations in both Nigeria and Peru. Many conditions of Shell's operations are similar in both countries — Shell's project is the largest single foreign investment in each country, both hydrocarbon projects are located in fragile tropical ecosystems inhabited by native peoples. Both areas have recently or are still experiencing extended periods of violence inflicted upon indigenous communities in the region of Shell operations. The concern is that Nigeria today could be Peru tomorrow.

Shell has failed to provide local indigenous communities with full environmental information about its operation. Shell began operations on indigenous lands without full community consultation. Moreover, the company will soon start to drill in a reserve set aside for the protection of nomadic, uncontacted peoples. Shell has left open the option to build roads into this remote rainforest area and will dump drilling wastes into the Amazon environment. Neither of these operating practices rank among top environmental standards.

Shell Nigeria never told the Niger Delta peoples about the environmental impact that its operations would have, never consulted the local peoples and has operated in a manner that has devastated the environment. Shell Nigeria has not operated to internationally acceptable environmental standards for the past forty years. Furthermore, Shell has intentionally turned communities against each other, paid and provided logistical support and arms for the Nigerian military, and bribed witnesses to testify against environmental activists. No one expects Shell to solve all of Nigeria's problems — just stop contributing to them.

Source: Project Underground's independent annual report "Human Rights and Environmental Operations Information on the Royal Dutch Shell Group of Companies, 1996-1997."

Some will provide electricity; others will distribute it; and still others will act as brokers, hooking up each office building, factory or apartment complex

Dams Across America

Dams have long been promoted as a major way to create low cost, safe, pollution free electricity. But their environmental implications have been ruinous:

Dams in U.S.:	80,000
Dams built by Corps of Engineers & Bureau of Reclamation:	750
Dams considered "unsafe":	2,500
Acres of land under man-made reservoirs:	12 million acres
Longest free-flowing stretch of Columbia River:	47 miles[1]
Only large river in lower 48 states without a dam:	Yellowstone
% U.S. electricity generated by hydropower:	10 percent
% juvenile salmon killed by dams on Snake and Columbia rivers:	95 percent
Dams blocking New England salmon runs:	900
Reduction in Atlantic salmon population from pre-dam levels:	99 percent
First dam to be dynamited to save fish:	Grangeville[2]
Cost of dams due to lost salmon fisheries (1960–1990):	$8 billion

[1] *through the Hanford Nuclear Reservation*
[2] *55-foot-tall dam on the Clearwater River in Idaho (1963)*

JAMES RIDGEWAY

The Bonneville dam is one of the biggest salmon-killing dams on the Columbia River.

with the best producer. So, if a landlord in the Bronx wants to make the cheapest deal, the energy broker can hook her or him up with a big electrical furnace in, say, British Columbia or Texas. If on the other hand, the landlord is worried about pollution and wants green energy then he or she can arrange to buy direct from a Working Assets-type producing company that makes electricity from wind energy outside Los Angeles or from solar panels in Arizona.

DEREGULATION—The illusion of better service at cheaper prices.

But so far this has turned out to be pure fantasy. In states like California and Massachusetts, deregulation has resulted in well organized groups of large industrial consumers negotiating good prices for themselves, while leaving small businesses and residential consumers with the same high prices and the real prospects of having to pay for the big utility's stranded costs built through years of boondoggles in nuclear and other inefficient energy schemes. ☠

John E. Bryson
CEO Edison International

SALARY:
$1.9 million

AGE:
54

EDUCATION:
Stanford and Yale Law Schools

BUSINESS PROFILE:
former chair of California Public Utilities Commission, state Water Resources Control Board

BEST DEAL WHEELED:
$26 billion ratepayer-financed bail-out of California electric utilities deregulation

MOST IMAGINATIVE SIDELINE:
co-founding Natural Resources Defense Fund

AP/WIDE WORLD PHOTOS

NOTABLE FACT:
In addition to the company's nuclear plant, nearly 15 percent of its electricity is generated by a coal-fired plant at Laughlin, Nevada. The plant, which is equipped with minimal pollution control devices, is notorious for having some of the worst emissions in the nation. Its smoke shrouds the Grand Canyon, and its generators are fired by coal stripped off Black Mesa on the Navajo reservation by Peabody Coal. Subsidiary Mission Energy snagged lucrative deals to build filthy coal-fired plants in Indonesia.

QUOTABLE QUOTE:
"Mexico is now on its way to achieving the economic prosperity that will allow it to afford greater environmental efforts . . . but it can achieve that prosperity only with expanded electrification," after planning the construction of Carbon II, one of the hemisphere's dirtiest coal-fired plant projects just over the border in Mexico. Amid controversy, the company eventually pulled out of the plant project.

ANNUAL SALES
$20 billion

HEADQUARTERS
Houston, TX

CEO/SALARY
Kenneth L. Lay
$2.6 million

**POLITICAL
CONTRIBUTIONS**
• $615,000

PRODUCTS
• natural gas
• electric power plants

MAJOR CUSTOMERS
• electric utilities

ENVIRONMENTAL RAPSHEET

• Enron faces regulatory problems in disposing of hazardous waste, gas processing facilities, as well as for facilities in Iowa as well as Florida.

• In Puerto Rico, an Enron subsidiary which supplies propane through underground pipes was harshly criticized by the National Transportation Safety Board for a 1996 explosion that killed 33 people, injured 69 others, destroyed a six-story commercial building, and damaged surrounding structures. The NTSB noted that Enron had known for more than 10 years that its subsidiary's operations did not comply with pipeline safety requirements, but failed to make the San Juan firm comply. The NTSB also found that the company's employees missed—and thus did not repair—gas leaks because "neither employee training or supervision were adequate." Survivors have filed 250 lawsuits.

OTHER POINTS OF INTEREST

• Enron is the leading supplier of natural gas to electric utilities in the U.S. as well as power and pipeline projects in a dozen countries, and has recently entered the utility business in Oregon and California.

• Enron also participates in the wind energy business.

DISHONORABLE MENTION

Oil Companies

EXXON is the world's largest oil company and the second largest company (after General Motors) in the world with more than $150 billion in annual sales. But it is also one of the foulest. Its lineage stretches directly back to John D. Rockefeller. He spawned Exxon, formerly Standard Oil of New Jersey; Chevron, formerly Standard Oil of California; Mobil, formerly Standard Oil of New York; and Amoco, formerly Standard Oil of Indiana. Standard Oil of New Jersey was the core of the Rockefeller oil empire.

In the treatment of the environment, of its workers, and customers, Exxon operates as if it were immune from any regulatory constraint. Most notoriously, its tanker the Exxon Valdez discharged 11 million gallons of crude oil into Prince William Sound after running aground in 1989. Perhaps the company's most brazen effrontery in the affair was to recycle some of the $5 billion in damages owed to Alaska's fishing industry back into its own coffers. The judge called Exxon's actions "a repugnant secret deal."

Exxon's air pollution record at its refineries is one of the worst in the business with hundreds of citations. Moreover, it refuses to disclose the toxic chemicals used at its refineries outside the U.S., and at many sites inside the country. The company was charged in 1992 with defrauding the Defense Department when it falsified records in order to help its oil additives qualify for military contracts. Exxon agreed to pay $3.8 million in fines.

From 1988 to 1992, OSHA issued 41 citations against Exxon that it termed serious and willful violations of worker safety rules. Although Exxon has a prominority reputation, only 11 percent of Exxon's managers are women and only 12 percent are minorities. Until 1995, there were no women or blacks among the 18 top corporate officers.

Exxon is making huge investments in developing nations where its record on environmental and human rights issues is less than stellar. One particularly ugly project is in eastern Venezuela, where Exxon has joined with the Venezuela national oil company to develop a $3 billion natural gas reserve deep in the rainforest, where it destroys rainforests, encroaches on indigenous lands, and spouts leaks.

TEXACO has a grim corporate history. During the late 1930s the company made millions by illegally shipping oil and gas to Mussolini and Hitler. Its president, Thorkild Rieber, was forced to resign his position after sympathetic statements about the Nazis were exposed by Texaco employees.

Texaco's racist attitude toward its minority employees forced the company to recently settle a class action suit for a record $176 million. The company is deeply involved in Indonesia and Siberia and was one of the big cheerleaders of the Gulf War because 60 percent of its refinery output depended on Saudi and Kuwaiti crude oil.

SHELL. Texaco has merged its U.S. refining and sales with Shell, the U.S. subsidiary of Royal Dutch/Shell Group, the world's second largest oil company. The most recent blot on Shell's copybook was its successful urging of the Nigerian government to deal summarily with Ken Saro-Wiwa, who was inconveniencing Shell by organizing protests against the company's operations in the Ogoni tribal lands along the Niger River and in the Niger's delta. The Nigerian government promptly arrested Saro-Wiwa and his fellow activists and hanged them six months later. Not only did Shell conspicuously refuse to join the international campaign to save Saro-Wiwa and the eight other activists (19 more are still in death cells), but it has been forced to ad-

Ken Saro-Wiwa

mit that the company armed mobile police units operating in the Ogoni region. The *London Observer* reported that "in 1990 the mobile police whose nickname in Nigeria is the Kill and Go Mob killed 15 in the village of

Umuechem, where Shell installations were being attacked by villagers angry at the pollution." Subsequently a company spokesman admitted that the company had bought arms for police guarding Shell's oil rigs in the Ogoni region.

Shell has a particularly awful poison rap sheet. It is one of the world's leading producers of pesticides. It co-ran operations at the Rocky Mountain Arsenal, where nerve gas was produced for the U.S. Army and pesticides for the agricultural industry. One of the pesticides concocted there was dibromochloropropane (DBCP), the use of which was banned in the U.S. because it caused sterility in farm workers. Undeterred, Shell exported large amounts of DBCP to Costa Rica and Honduras, where more than 13,000 workers later claimed they had been sterilized after having come in contact with the chemical.

ARCO. The Atlantic Richfield Company is one of the big despoilers of the Alaskan tundra, where 66 percent of Arco's domestic reserves are located. It was in 1968 that Arco tapped the largest oil deposit in North America, on Alaska's North Slope. The company's treatment of the fragile Arctic ecosystem has been dreadful, with toxic wastes dumped into 200 pits dug into the tundra wetlands. Arco has been responsible for numerous spills along the Trans-Alaska pipeline. When six employees of Alyeska Pipeline Services (the company that runs the pipeline and is co-owned by Arco, BP, and Exxon) uncovered charges of mismanagement and illegal dumping, they were harassed, intimidated, and fired. After a judge ruled the employees to be whistleblowers protected by federal law, they were offered their jobs back and substantial financial settlements. In 1990 Arco's chemical plant in Channelview, Texas, exploded, killing 17 workers. OSHA later cited the company for 347 safety code violations at the plant. Arco settled the matter by paying a $3.5 million fine.

Arco was one of the first companies to introduce reformulated gasoline, which has caused chronic health problems in areas where it is widely used, such as Alaska. The EPA has found high levels of poisonous methyl tertiary butyl ether (MTBE) in blood samples of Anchorage residents, who complain of persistent headaches and nausea.

CHEVRON. Sharing global operations with Texaco in a company called Caltex, Chevron is deep into Indonesia. Among its more notorious international operations was a close association with the former apartheid government in South Africa, where it remained active despite the international boycott. Chevron led the entry of oil drillers into Papua New Guinea, where Caltex's security forces murderously suppressed indigenous protests.

Inside the U.S., Chevron has a particularly appalling record of oil spills and toxic releases. In October of 1994 it was hit with the largest fine—$17 million—ever issued under the Toxic Substances Control Act, for fabricating data on the presence of toxic compounds in its detergent gasoline. Chevron called it "merely a paperwork oversight." Chevron has also repeatedly run afoul of the Clean Water Act, by dumping waste into wetlands, estuaries, and the Pacific Ocean. In 1986 its refinery at El Segundo, California, faced 888 citations for violations of the Act, resulting in a fine of $1.5 million. In 1992, the company was forced to plead guilty on 65 counts of violating the Act at a drilling rig in the Pacific. Chevron coughed up $6.5 million in fines and $1.5 million in civil penalties. The company's Richmond refinery is the largest water user in the parched area east of San Francisco Bay.

Chevron owns hundreds of leases to drill for oil along the Rocky Mountain front from Yellowstone National Park in Wyoming to Glacier Park in northern Montana. In order to protect these leases, Chevron has invested heavily in the "Wise Use" anti-environmental campaigns in the western states.

BP. Like Arco, British Petroleum is in Alaska, where its holdings yield more than half the company's annual output of crude oil. In November 1994, BP reached a $1.4 billion settlement for unpaid taxes on its North

Big Oil's Environmental Record

Slope oil, dating back to 1978. Its environmental record in Alaska is as bad as Arco's. In the lower 48 states, BP had big violations, too. For example, at a Pennsylvania refinery it incurred numerous citations for violating laws on the dumping of hazardous wastes, finally settling claims for $2.3 million. BP's record in the Latin American rain forests, where it's engaged in mining and drilling operations, has been widely and deservedly excoriated. The company has worked with the Colombian military in order to ensure unimpeded access to five trillion cubic feet of natural gas reserves the company has leases on. BP recently went through a particularly brutal downsizing, dumping 23 percent of its workers. Its proposed merger with Amoco will further concentrate the international oil industry.

PHILLIPS. In the 1940s the Oklahoma-based company was actually run by a Cherokee Indian, William Keeler, aka Tsula Westa Nehi. Keeler helped Phillips make a lot of money by drilling on native lands, a practice the company has zestfully engaged in ever since. (Keeler, however, was the first and, to date, only minority officer of the company.) Phillips stepped eagerly into Indonesia not long after Suharto and the generals were assisted by the CIA in identifying and killing upward of a million people suspected of being communists or their sympathizers. Since 1989 the company has been drilling in the Timor Gap, off the coast of East Timor. On its board is Lawrence Eagleburger, who was Henry Kissinger's aide and Undersecretary of State when Kissinger, with President Ford, visited Jakarta in 1975, three days before the Indonesian invasion of East Timor. In 1989, a massive explosion occured at Phillip's chemical plant in Houston, killing 23 people.

Timber

N 1600 THE LANDS THAT ARE NOW THE United States contained nearly 1.1 billion acres of wild and unruly forest. It's said that the hardwood forests of the eastern United States—one of the most diverse ecosystems outside the tropics—were so dense with oak, maple, and beech trees that an intrepid squirrel could scamper from the Carolinas to the Mississippi River without ever touching ground. Four-fifths of the original American forests were located east of the Mississippi, with most of the heartland treeless plain and desert. Along the Pacific Coast, however, the cool and wet climate has nourished the most impressive forest on the planet. This coastal forest, stretching from the Sierras in California to southeast Alaska, harbors the oldest, tallest, and largest trees on Earth.

The Puritans called the primeval forest they encountered in America a "green Hell." The great American woods were viewed by the likes of Cotton

Mather as an obstacle to both settlement and the practice of religion. There was certainly nothing to compare to these vast woodlands back in England

---

Man-Made Disaster Areas

In 1980, President Jimmy Carter boarded a helicopter in Portland, Oregon, to view the damage caused by the eruption of Mt. St. Helens. As the aircraft approached the southern rim of the volcano, the President turned to one of his guides and said that he had never seen such devastation. The guide informed the president that the plane was not yet over the blast zone and that the land he was viewing was the Gifford Pinchot National Forest, which had been extensively clearcut by local timber companies.

---

or continental Europe. By the time the Mayflower set sail for Plymouth, nearly 90 percent of England's forests had already been wiped out and the Black Forest of Germany had been turned into a manicured woodlot by Bavarian forest meisters. And European settlers quickly set about re-creating this state of affairs in the New World.

Timber—A Strategic Resource

If the Puritans saw the American forest as an impediment, the British Navy seized upon the American forest as a vital strategic resource. In 1689 Brit-

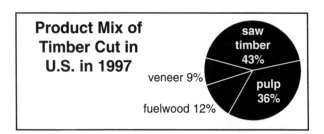

Product Mix of Timber Cut in U.S. in 1997

saw timber 43%

pulp 36%

veneer 9%

fuelwood 12%

JOHN SCHOEN

Tongass old growth trees.

ain decreed that all lands capable of producing masts and other materials be reserved for the Royal Navy as "naval stores." In New England, patches of forest were reserved for the production of masts and shipbuilding timbers. In the pine forests of the South, turpentine, pitch, and tar were extracted, largely through slave labor. By 1700, conflicts began to develop between colonists and the British government over control of these reserves. The colonists wanted the timber resources for their own shipbuilding needs and to supply a lucrative timber trade with the West Indies. This little reported conflict was a driving factor behind the American Revolution.

The first sawmill in the United States was constructed outside York, Maine, in 1623. By 1800 there were more than 1,000 sawmills in the young republic, churning out siding, flooring, and fence rails. From 1800 to 1900 the lumber industry was a dynamo of the

U.S. FOREST SERVICE

Tongass clearcut, 1992.

Fatality Rate	
(per 100,000 employed)	
loggers*	101
timber executives	2
*logging ranks highest of all major occupations	

American economy, accounting for nearly 6 percent of the national manufacturing product. For much of the nineteenth century forest products ranked as the second largest industry, right behind flour and grist mills. The industry was also one of the country's largest employers. Writing in 1836, James Hall called America "a wooden country." In fact, during the eighteenth and nineteenth centuries more than 70 percent of the timber logged was used not as building material, but as fuel to heat houses and power factories, railroad engines, and steamers. (Even today more than 40 percent of the wood cut in the northern states is for fuel.)

THE DEFORESTATION OF AMERICA

By 1880 nearly 400 million acres of the original American forest had been logged off. Around the

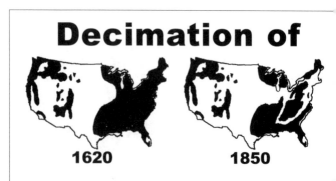

Decimation of

1620   1850

turn of the century, the pace of the logging became frenzied. From 1880 to about 1910, more than 8,300 acres of forest were cleared every day. By 1920, the original forest cover of the United States had been reduced by 65 percent to about 430 million acres.

Timber "harvesting" in the Ashley National Forest.

More than any other factor, the rapid pace of deforestation spurred the birth of the American conservation movement and the creation of the national forests. In the West, much of the forest land had

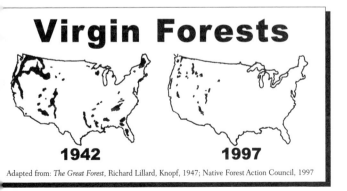

Virgin Forests

1942   **1997**

Adapted from: *The Great Forest*, Richard Lillard, Knopf, 1947; Native Forest Action Council, 1997

lain in the public domain, under the ownership and stewardship of the federal government. But the destruction of these public domain forests had been abetted by two disastrous laws: the Free Timber Act and the Timber and Stone Act, which sold off federal timber lands for only $1.25 an acre. Although the land was supposed to go to individuals as an incentive to settlement of the Western states, through

---

Too Many Trees?

In the summer of 1997, Wheelabrator, a California technology firm, began handing out brochures at environmental gatherings with the eye-grabbing headline: "The problem: too many trees. The solution: biomass." The slick brochure claims that overstocked stands of forests in the West pose a fire risk. The company proposes logging off these stands of trees and burning the logs in small wood-fueled energy plants built by Wheelabrator. This is the meeting ground of timber policy and the move toward energy deregulation. The company is urging environmentalists to support millions of dollars in subsidies to log forests in northern California and have the wood delivered to Wheelabrator-built energy plants in the West. The company would also earn millions in state-sponsored credits as an "alternative energy producer." The irony is Wheelabrator stands poised to reap millions for a plan that leaves ecological scars on the forest and emits greenhouse gasses that will accelerate global warming trends.

> Company to environmentalists: Support our effort to log off forests in order to reduce forest fire danger.

---

a variety of complex schemes and swindles, much of the land ended up in the clutches of a few large timber firms, the so-called logging trusts of the late 1880s. To stem this tide and counter the overcutting

U.S. timber being shipped to Japan from export docks at Longivew, WA.

of the western forests, Congress passed a series of laws in the 1890s setting aside 170 million acres of public lands as "forest reserves." These lands became the backbone of the national forest system.

The early conservation movement, championed by Teddy Roosevelt, was no enemy to big business; it simply sought to preserve select wild lands while organizing the disposal of resources in the name of "efficiency." And in fact, the big timber syndicates supported the creation of the national forests. The reason was simple: taking 200 million acres of forest off the market drove up the value of their own holdings. These companies were content to forgo logging on the national forests until the post-World War II housing boom in the early 1950s. Then, with their own lands largely depleted by decades of aggressive logging, the big timber companies urged the Forest Service to open the national forests to industrial logging.

Diversification

The timber market is wildly erratic, with prices of lumber and pulp fluctuating as much as 75 percent over a six-month period. As a result many of the big companies have branched out into entirely new areas of operation.

• Weyerhaeuser, the self-styled "tree growing people," now operates a financial services and mortgage division that generates over a billion dollars in business a year.

• Kimberly-Clark owns its own airline company.

• Maxxam, the company which owns the largest stand of red-woods in the world, also owns Kaiser Aluminum and dog racing tracks in Texas and Puerto Rico.

• James River, a leading producer of cardboard boxes and copy-ing paper, also is the largest producer of plastic knives.

• International Paper, the behemoth of the timber business, earns nearly $4 billion a year from its oil and gas reserves, pho-tographic film and chemicals.

There are also many other firms which own a stake in the timber business.

• The Universal Corporation, the nation's leading producer of tobacco, operates a profitable hardwood lumber division.

• The John Hancock Insurance Company owns nearly 500,000 acres of timber land and is a leading log exporter.

• The Washington Post Company and Dow Jones are the co-owners of the Bear Island Timber Company, which controls about 500,000 acres in South Carolina.

The Forest Service complied. From 1955 through 1990, it allowed nearly 800,000 acres a year of public forest to be logged off at discount rates, largely through clearcutting. To allow access to those timber sales, the Forest Service became the world's biggest road construction firm, building more than 365,000 miles of roads in less than 40 years and passing on the bills to taxpayers. The agency now maintains a road net-work eight times the size of the interstate highway system, only one of many effective government subsidies to an already profitable industry.

The Timber Wars

Then in 1991 the spotted owl, a denizen of the

Regrowth vs. Old Growth

In 1993, on the eve of President Clinton's summit on forest policy held in Portland, Oregon, the timber industry launched a $50 million public relations campaign, featuring full-page ads and television spots. The campaign was titled, "The Truth About America's Forests." It said

[T]oday America has over 20 percent more trees than it had just 20 years ago. And the numbers are growing daily, with trees being replenished faster than they are harvested in every region of the country. Thanks, in part, to private landowners and America's forest products companies, who plant over 6,000,000 trees a day, re-seed entire forests and use other forest management techniques to promote natural regrowth. We're determined to keep up with the growing demand for wood and paper products. And to make sure our forests are a continuing source of joy for every American.

In fact, while the amount of land covered by trees has increased since the turn of the century due to the reforestation of marginal agricultural land, these plantations can hardly be considered forests, since the trees are mowed down every 15 to 20 years. The more relevant comparison is between the number of trees larger than three feet in diameter (or about 100 years old). In the past 20 years, America has lost nearly 10 million acres of these old-growth trees.

Replanting figures are similarly misleading for two reasons. Studies in Montana and Idaho have shown that more than 60 percent of the trees replanted after clearcutting die less than five years after planting. Second, it will take the replanted trees nearly 200 years of growth to replace the

> It would appear that the timber industry sees no difference between Christmas tree farms and old growth forests.

ecological value of the 500- to 1,000-year-old trees that were logged off.

old growth forests of the Pacific Northwest, was listed as a threatened species. A federal judge ordered the Forest Service to drastically scale back logging in the bird's forest habitat and, as a result, by 1995 Forest Service timber sale volumes had plummeted to levels not seen since the 1930s. The log-

Smokey's Fatal Mistake

In the 1930s the biggest fear of timber companies such as Weyerhaeuser was that a wildfire would sweep across their lands and destroy billions of dollars worth of trees. As insurance against this calamity, the timber barons' lobbyists convinced the U.S. Forest Service to pursue an aggressive fire suppression policy. The Forest Service soon adopted a plan of putting out every wildfire "by 10 AM." It also developed a national advertising campaign featuring Smokey the Bear, who soon became the most popular advertising character in history. Congress funded the program lavishly, often to the tune of more than $1 billion a year. A historian of the Forest Service once observed that the agency fought fires by "throwing money on them."

> Decades of fire suppression severely altered the ecology of these forests.

But in fact the Forest Service was too successful in its mission. Most of the western forests evolved with regular fires that cleansed the forest of dying and dead trees. Decades of fire suppression severely altered the ecology of these forests, allowing massive amounts of dead wood to accumulate on the forest floor, providing a nesting ground for forest-killing insects and diseases. By the early 1990s millions of acres of forest in the West were threatened not by fire, but by the exclusion of fire. The timber industry offered a typical solution: clearcut the ailing forests even faster in patterns that might "mimic" wildfires.

Arson was the predictable result of the Forest Service's habit of scheduling salvage timber sales after forest fires. In Oregon and Idaho, loggers set large-scale fires in forest lands that were otherwise protected from logging. In Arizona a Forest Service ranger was convicted of arson after setting a fire in an old-growth stand on the Kaibab National Forest.

Comparison of Average Wages

	annual	hourly
Sawmill worker	$15,000	$7
Logger	$17,000	$8
Pulpmill worker	$23,000	$11
Ex-vice president	$635,000	$294
Director's Fees*	$40,000	$333
CEO	$1,330,000	$625

based on 120 hours of meetings & travel

ging didn't stop, of course, much of it just shifted east to the rugged landscape of the northern Rockies, the lair of the grizzly bear and home to the last untrammeled wilderness in the lower 48 states. Even in Oregon and Washington the cutting of the big old trees only barely slowed. In the spring of 1996, for example, the Forest Service sold off for clearcutting more than 20,000 acres of forest, containing thousands of trees more than 500 hundred years old. These developments sparked the so-called Timber Wars, which pit-

The legendary spotted owl.

ted environmentalists against logging companies in sometimes violent face-offs.

Meanwhile, the nature of the American timber

industry had changed. The South had displaced the Pacific Northwest as the nation's biggest timber producing region. Increasingly, timber companies are choosing to chip entire trees into pulp for newsprint and so-called engineered wood products like particleboard instead of waiting an additional 20 to 30 years until the trees grow large enough to produce construction-quality wood. At the same time, U.S. timber companies are moving their mills to Mexico and exporting more and more of the higher quality timber as raw logs, thus eliminating American jobs.

Timber Pork

There are approximately 365,000 miles of federally built roads on the national forests—about eight times the size of the U.S. interstate highway system. The cost of constructing and maintaining these roads is equivalent to a subsidy to the timber industry of $200 million a year. *Each new mile* of road construction costs taxpayers as much as $50,000. The Forest Service plans to construct about 2000 miles of new road every year for the next decade, much of it in previously roadless land. These roads also contribute to the decline of the grizzly bear, an increase in landslides, and destruction of coastal salmon stocks.

How Taxpayers Subsidize Timber Production

• Each year Forest Service timber sales to private companies at below market rates cost U.S. taxpayers more than $500 million.

• For years Weyerhaeuser and other firms have enjoyed a $30 million tax break for exporting logs.

• In states where timber companies are the largest property owners, they pay the lowest property taxes to the states.

• One of the biggest subsidies to the timber industry is the Forest Service's fire suppression program, which basically functions as a $500 million fire insurance policy for timber companies in the West.

Pulp mill in coastal Oregon.

The legacy of the timber industry is a host of environmental problems. Deforestation has led to an increase in greenhouse gases, soil erosion, landslides, and decimation of trout and salmon habitats. In the rainy winter of 1996 the Mapleton Ranger District on the Siuslaw National Forest in coastal Oregon experienced over 180 landslides, nearly 80 percent of them originated in clearcuts or along logging roads. Pulp mills are a prime source of the deadly toxin dioxin.

Today less than 30 million acres of old growth forest remain, mostly on public lands. Fewer than five million acres of old growth exists on private and corporate-owned forest lands. Almost all of this is in small, isolated patches that do not function as forest ecosystems. By 1996, the U.S. was running a timber deficit, forests were being logged over faster than they were growing back, and Hall's "wooden country" was importing nearly twice as much timber as it was exporting. ☠

Bug Invasion

At the turn of the century, the majestic American chestnut tree filled up to 25 percent of the eastern forests and supported an entire complex ecosystem. By 1950, a rapidly spreading fungus—recently traced to a source in Japan—had virtually wiped out the chestnut. In the 1970s, the elm trees that lined the streets of New York City fell prey to Dutch Elm disease, a plague that spread westward and destroyed two-thirds of the nation's elms. The apparent source of the disease was a single imported log, which rode the rails west from New York through Pennsylvania and into Ohio.

Today, scientists are in a panic over the threat to another abundant American species, the maple. The source of all their worries is a small, spotted bug found crawling out of a Brooklyn maple tree. The discovery of the Asian Long Horn Beetle—brought in,

> When these new diseases are brought into the U.S., they can destroy not only species, but whole ecosystems.

this time, from China—has led some scientists to call for a preemptive strike that would cost the borough's streets and parks all of its maple trees. It has also brought home questions about loosening environmental regulations in a time of unrestricted international trade.

More than 800 million trees in New York, covering 62 percent of the state's 18 million acres of forested land, are possible targets of the bug. Potential losses could run into the billions of dollars.

Unfortunately, the discovery of the Brooklyn bug presages a much broader threat to America's already dwindling forests. The Asian Long Horn Beetle is just one of a new wave of invading pests and diseases with names like the Asian gypsy moth and the pine bark beetle and the Mexican canker, brought to American shores in increasing numbers as the result of increased—and increasingly unregulated—foreign trade. Many of these exotic insects and fungi are carried on logs that have been cut down by international companies that are searching out wood supplies in the heart of the world's few remaining primal forests. "One of the real problems," says Fields Cobb, Jr., a University of California forest pathologist, "is that as we start logging off the natural forests of the tropics and other remote areas it will be very easy to overlook potentially dangerous pests and diseases. These disease-causing agents are very obscure in their native habitat, because natural forests in diverse ecosystems tend to suppress widespread pest outbreaks." When these new diseases are brought into the U.S., they can destroy not only species, but whole ecosystems. The chestnut, for example, "was an unsurpassed source of food for wildlife," says Cobbs. "Dozens of species depended on it, including the bald eagle." In addition, Cobbs notes, the place of the chestnut tree was taken by oaks of lesser quality, which opened the way to the emergence of another deadly disease called oak wilt, now threatening all the oaks in the eastern forests, and making the eastern forests much more susceptible to ravages of the gypsy moths.

> These disease-causing agents are very obscure in their native habitat, because natural forests in diverse ecosystems tend to suppress widespread pest outbreaks.

These logs are coming to the U.S. in steadily increasing numbers to replace supplies of American timber, which have been diminished by overcutting—and, ironically, by an increase in American logs being shipped overseas due to the loosening of environmentally related trade rules under both GATT and NAFTA. And yet another threat looms just over the horizon in the prospect of an enormous import program involving hundreds of companies anxious to import timber from Siberia. In this vast territory, where the timber is controlled by the Russian Mafia and the logging done by prison gangs, the bugs are rampant. A USDA team reported in 1991, "this assessment clearly demonstrates that the risk of significant impacts to North American forests is great," running anywhere from $25 million in the best of circumstances to $58 *billion* in a worst case scenario.

The U.S. banned the import of raw Siberian logs in 1990, citing among other things the threat to the Douglas fir by the Asian gypsy moth or the Spruce bark beetle. Then, in 1994 it proposed new rules that would effectively drop the ban.

■■■ Spotted Owls, Profits, and Jobs ■■■

In 1991, the northern spotted owl was listed as a threatened species and federal judge William Dwyer ordered a halt to logging on national forest lands occupied by the owl. The Northwest Forestry Association, an industry trade group, loudly proclaimed that each spotted owl pair would cost the timber industry more than $2 million. The predictions proved wildly inaccurate. Instead of ruining the industry, the spotted owl controversy sparked an unprecedented stream of profits for the nation's biggest timber companies. The rea-

> **The spotted owl controversy sparked unprecedented profits for the biggest timber companies.**

son was simple: the reduction in timber volume logged from the national forests due to measures to protect the owl and other endangered species sharply increased the value of timber. For example, the price of Douglas fir rose from $450 per thousand board feet in 1989 to more than $900 in 1994. In 1987, the year the national forests set a record for amount of timber it sold, the eight largest timber companies in the United States earned a combined $2.1 billion in profits. By 1995, however, when the national forests sold the least volume of timber since World War II, the profits of these same firms rose to an astounding $4.8 billion.

Another issue was jobs. The American Forest and Paper Association claimed that reductions in logging to protect wildlife would ravage the economies of the Northwest, costing the region more than 100,000 jobs. But the industry experienced its greatest job loss during the period when it was logging record amounts of timber. From 1980 to 1990, the industry saw a decline of about 15 percent of its workforce, even though it was cutting 6 percent more timber than it had in 1979. During that period, Oregon saw a loss of 12,000 timber industry jobs, but total employment in the state rose by more than 160,000 jobs. Similar trends are found in other western states. Where did the timber industry jobs go? Some of them were lost to automation and the upgrading of outdated sawmills and machinery. But most of the jobs were lost to the export of raw logs, as big timber firms such as Weyerhaeuser and Georgia-Pacific cashed in on high prices to sell logs to the Japanese without running them through U.S. sawmills. This U.S. export of raw logs cost American millworkers 30,000 jobs.

BAD GUY PROFILE:

Charles Hurwitz
CEO, Maxxam

AGE:
61

NICKNAME:
Charlie Hustle

EDUCATION:
University of Texas

BUSINESS PROFILE:
Maxxam is a Houston-based holding company that Hurwitz used to launch his takeover of Pacific Lumber, the California firm which owns the largest stand of redwoods in the world. After the takeover, Hurwitz ordered the company to triple the rate of logging in order to pay off the Michael Milken junk bonds used to finance the raid. In less than 10 years, more than 80,000 acres of redwoods were leveled, leaving behind only the 10,000-acre Headwaters grove.

BEST DEAL WHEELED:
In 1996, Hurwitz convinced the Clinton administration to support a taxpayer financed buyout of the Headwaters grove for $380 million, even though companies he controls owe the federal treasury nearly $2 billion for the collapse of the Houston-based United Savings and Loan. Hurwitz restructured his company so that instead of the funds going to pay down the company's massive debt, it goes directly to a partnership controlled by Hurwitz. A GAO study conducted in the summer of 1997 revealed that the market value of Headwaters was less than $100 million.

MOST IMAGINATIVE SIDELINE:
Hurwitz plans to build dog racing tracks in Puerto Rico.

NOTABLE FACT:
Hurwitz is the only figure involved in the takeover of Pacific Lumber not to be indicted. Milken, Ivan Boesky, and Boyd Jeffries all served time for their role in the hostile takeover.

QUOTABLE QUOTE:
"I follow the golden rule. He who has the gold, rules."

INTERNATIONAL Ⓐ PAPER

ANNUAL SALES
$20 billion

HEADQUARTERS
Purchase, NY

CEO/SALARY
John Dillon
$3.2 million

PRODUCTS
• printing paper
• industrial packaging
• fibreboard
• export logs
• lumber
• linerboard
• pulp

POLITICAL CONTRIBUTIONS
• $300,000

LOBBY FEES
• $1,200,000

ENVIRONMENTAL RAPSHEET

• International Paper is one of the major polluters in "cancer alley," along the lower reaches of the Mississippi River; its four plants pour millions of gallons of dioxin tainted water into the river every day.
• International Paper logs on incredibly short rotations, allowing its trees to grow for only 15 years.
• It is the leading importer of raw logs from New Zealand that may carry dangerous exotic pests and diseases.

OTHER POINTS OF INTEREST

• Long backed by Rockefeller cash, IP now reigns as the world's largest timber company and continues a global buying spree, acquiring firms in New Zealand, Chile, Mexico and China.
• Maintained a long relationship with Clinton, securing favorable tax treatment for its pulp mill in Pine Bluff.
• Provided the Whitewater Development Corporation with land for the Whitewater deals.
• Formed partnership with the Nature Conservancy to promote voluntary compliance with environmental laws.

BAD GUY PROFILE:

ANNUAL SALES
$12 billion

HEADQUARTERS
Tacoma, WA

CEO/SALARY
John Creighton
$1 million

PRODUCTS
• newsprint
• bleached paper
• chips
• plywood
• pulp
• lumber
• export logs

POLITICAL CONTRIBUTIONS
• $86,000

LOBBY FEES
• $510,000

ENVIRONMENTAL RAPSHEET

• Weyerhaeuser owns the most productive forest land in the Pacific Northwest, lowland temperate rainforest packed with Douglas fir and Western cedar. Its rapacious logging over the past 50 years has largely eliminated old growth forest from more than two million acres, making it the largest single destroyer of the habitat of the northern spotted owl.
• Deeply invested in production of tree clones at its numerous "tree farms."
• Its pulp mills in Longview, Washington and Plymouth, North Carolina are among the nation's most toxic plants.
• Pled guilty in 1997 to killing endangered hawks.

OTHER POINTS OF INTEREST

• Weyerhaeuser is the aristocracy of the American timber industry dating back to late 1800s.
• The company acquired nearly treeless Mt. Rainier which it traded to federal government for a million acres of the world's most productive forest.
• Brought former EPA director William Ruckleshaus onto the board in late 1980s.
• Formed an exclusive timber capital fund to finance operations in China, Siberia, and South America.

GEORGIA-PACIFIC

ANNUAL SALES
$13 billion

PRODUCTS
• building materials
• office paper
• checks
• envelopes
• paper towels

CEO/SALARY
Alston D. Correll
$2.1 million

HEADQUARTERS
Atlanta, GA

POLITICAL CONTRIBUTIONS
• $270,000

LOBBY FEES
• $70,000

ENVIRONMENTAL RAPSHEET
• GP epitomized cut-and-run logging, as it clearcut more than a million acres of forest in the Pacific Northwest with minimal investment in reforestation. Many GP clearcuts in Oregon remain nearly barren, 30 years after having been logged.
• Its top six pulp mills generate more than eight million tons of toxic pollutants every year.
• One of the nation's largest users of chemical pesticides, spraying thousands of gallons a year on its nearly six million acres of forest lands in the U.S.

OTHER POINTS OF INTEREST
•GP dominated for decades by its CEO, Owen Cheatham, a notorious racist, who adorned his office with a Confederate flag. Cheatham made millions off World War II when he arranged for his company to be the largest supplier of lumber to the U.S. military.
• Used its wartime profits to gobble up dozens of companies, ultimately attracting the attention of the Federal Trade Commission, which forced the company to spin off 20 percent of its land and mills, thus creating Louisiana-Pacific.
• Pled guilty in 1991 to tax evasion and was fined $5 million. Then hired former EPA director Lee Thomas as its VP for Environmental Affairs.

Timber Companies

CHAMPION INTERNATIONAL logged more than 500,000 acres in Montana in less than 10 years, contributing to the decline of the grizzly bear, wolf, and bull trout. The company was sued by citizens of Canton, North Carolina, for $5 billion in 1993 for flushing dioxin into Pigeon River. In 1996, a massive landslide started in a Champion clearcut on excessively steep lands in the Oregon coast mountain range. The landslide crushed a house, killing four people.

WILLAMETTE INDUSTRIES, the world's leading producer of brown paper bags, is infamous in environmental circles for its involvement in the "Easter Massacre" of 1987, when the company violated a federal judge's order and logged off the oldest trees in Oregon on Easter weekend.

KIMBERLY CLARK controls about a million acres of forest land in the U.S., which it logs at a savage pace, often cutting trees that are only 15 years old which it churns into pulp to make Kotex pads. The company is facing potentially crippling lawsuits over its sale of cigarette papers to the tobacco industry. Kimberly Clark also inherited a lawsuit over the role of Scott Paper in the manufacture of breast implants. The company's 1995 annual report informed shareholders of a new marketing possibility: "adult incontinence is on the rise," meaning increased demand for the company's Depends and Poise.

STONE CONTAINER, the world's leading producer of container board, cardboard boxes and newsprint, has one of the worst environmental records—illegally dumped toxic wastewater into two Arizona desert lakes; sued by Florida for contaminating groundwater, illegally dumped hazardous waste, and altered waste shipment records; sued by the EPA for violating its air permit in Montana and for illegally tampering with air pollution control equipment.

LOUISIANA-PACIFIC CORPORATION, one of the most fined companies in the U.S.; was investigated for theft of trees from the Tongass National Forest; the subject of civil suits in at least three states; sued for illnesses caused by aerial spraying of pesticides in California; logged off priceless stands of ancient redwoods in the late 1970s; gets more direct federal subsidies than any other timber company.

Timber Barons

RED EMMERSON, the largest private landowner in the United States, has ruled Sierra-Pacific Industries for the past 40 years by ruthlessly exerting his dominance in northern California and driving dozens of smaller mills and timber firms out of business. In the summer of 1997, Emmerson convinced California Senator Dianne Feinstein to push through Congress a law mandating that the national forests of northern California more than double the amount of timber it puts up for sale. Since Emmerson's company will be the only firm bidding, Sierra-Pacific is sure to get the timber for the minimum price, ensuring the old-time timber baron of millions in profits. He also funds "biological" research suggesting that spotted owls and salmon thrive in clearcuts.

ROGER STONE, CEO of Stone Container, took over the family company in 1975 and promptly began a buying spree backed by his pal Michael Milken's junk bonds, plunging the company into massive debt. At the same time Stone was slashing jobs at its U.S. plants, the company began to relocate to the third world, building mills and cardboard plants in Venezuela, Mexico, and China. He earned $3.2 million the same year his company lost $320 million.

AL DUNLAP, former CEO of Scott Paper, one of America's oldest and most conservative timber companies. After losing $280 million in 1993, because of a downturn in paper and pulp prices, Scott Paper hired Al Dunlap, who immediately fired 11,000 workers, logged off the last of the company's old-growth timber, sold off most of the company's mills and forest land (and eventually, the company itself to Kimberly-Clark), moved its factories to Mexico, and returned the company to profitability. Dunlap, himself, made nearly $100 million in 1995.

Hard-Rock Mining

HE CRUSTY MINER ARMED with a pickax and a mule is the very image of rugged individualism. Western expansion was spurred by such myths, as wave after wave of men headed to California, Colorado, and Idaho at the news of the latest gold or silver strike. In reality, of course, mining was dangerous work for little pay and most of the enormous profits ended up in the hands of eastern industrialists and robber barons, such as Jay Gould.

Hard-rock mining in the U.S. today continues to be controlled by a mere handful of companies. (For a discussion of coal mining, see the Energy chapter.) And many of the most lucrative mines in the U.S. are owned by Canadian or South African companies, such as Barrick, Noranda, Echo Bay, and

Minorco. Skirting anti-trust laws such as the Sherman Act, the big mining companies increasingly have begun to embark on cooperative ventures, where often as many as five large firms join together to operate a single site.

Mining over history has been among the very most destructive environmental enterprises on the planet. It is certainly the beneficiary of the most lax environmental laws, typified by the Mining Law of 1872. For more than 125 years, this law has been impervious to change. It offers up mineral-rich public lands for sale to mining companies for as little as $5 an acre, charges no royalties

> Mining has been among the most destructive environmental enterprises on the planet.

A River of Lead

The Coeur d'Alene River in northern Idaho flows through an area known as the Silver Valley, one of the world's most heavily mined landscapes. For more than four decades, toxic heavy metals have leached out of crushed rocks and other mine wastes from dozens of mines in the region ending up in the river. The Coeur d'Alene River flows into Lake Coeur d'Alene, one of the most scenic lakes in North America. But both the lake and the river are as deadly as they are beautiful. The bottom of Lake Coeur d'Alene is larded with mercury, cadmium, zinc, and lead. The lead levels in the both the lake and the river are six times the federal standard and pose severe health risks to humans, fish, and migratory birds, such as the Trumpeter swans that stop on the lake each spring and fall. The mining industry claims that the lake will naturally flush itself clean and that agriculture and logging pose bigger threats. The toxic debris is slowly moving into the Spokane River and toward the Columbia. The U.S. Geological Survey estimates that an additional 700 million tons of toxic mining waste may collapse into the Coeur d'Alene watershed over the next two decades.

Holding Yellowstone Hostage

On the northeast border of Yellowstone National Park, Noranda, a Canadian-owned mining conglomerate, bought up mineral rights to several thousands on Henderson Mountain, a 9,000-foot tall peak on national forest lands in Montana. The company soon announced plans to excavate a mammoth mine on the site. The called it the New World Mine. The proposal sparked an international uproar, condemnation on the editorial pages of the *New York Times* and a flurry of law suits. While the mining company pressed forward with its ambitious plans for the mine, it also hired Birch Bayh, a former Democratic senator from Indiana with close ties to the Clinton White House, to begin secret negotiations on a possible buyout plan. The mining company paid Bayh more than $125,000 for his service. It paid off. Prior to the 1996 Democratic convention, President Clinton journeyed to Yellowstone to announce a deal on the New World Mine. The mining company would be given $65 million for its mineral rights to the site, rights originally purchased from the federal government for less than $15,000. In addition, the government agreed to drop all legal actions against the firm. Sensing a profitable strategy, a few weeks later a small Wyoming firm filed more than 100 mining claims along the Rocky Mountain Front near Glacier National Park. The company demanded that the feds buy up its leases or they would proceed with plans to scar the landscape with strip mines.

---

for minerals exhumed from those lands, and contains no provisions for environmental restoration. The Mining Law, enacted by President Ulysses S. Grant, has given birth to some of the most lucrative financial deals in history. For example, in 1994 the Canadian company Barrick Resources paid the U.S. Department of Interior $10,000 for land containing an estimated $10 billion worth of gold.

Perhaps more than any other industry, mining has been characterized by wildly fluctuating boom-and-bust cycles. The ghost towns of the American

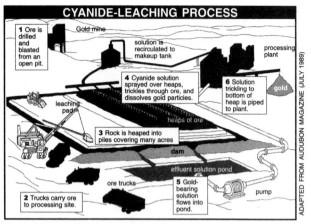

ADAPTED FROM AUDUBON MAGAZINE (JULY 1989)

CYANIDE-LEACHING PROCESS

Gold mine

1 Ore is drilled and blasted from an open pit.

solution is recirculated to makeup tank

processing plant

4 Cyanide solution sprayed over heaps, trickles through ore, and dissolves gold particles.

6 Solution trickling to bottom of heap is piped to plant.

gold

leaching pad

heaps of ore

3 Rock is heaped into piles covering many acres

dam

effluent solution pond

5 Gold-bearing solution flows into pond.

pump

2 Trucks carry ore to processing site.

ore trucks

This diagram illustrates the process of using cyanide to leach gold from ore.

West are almost uniformly mining towns that briefly flourished then suddenly collapsed.

The evidence is also written on the land, where more than 550,000 abandoned mines are spread across the country, many of them leaking highly toxic

PHILIP M. HOCKER/MINERAL POLICY CENTER

Cyanide leach gold mining at the Carlin Trend, Nevada.

waste into the nation's lakes and rivers. These mines have already poisoned more than 12,000 miles of streams. The vast Berkeley Pit, operated by Anaconda Copper, now contains 44 billion gallons of highly acidic water. The water level is rising so fast that the 1,000-foot deep pit will be breached in less than 10 years. Depressed prices for copper and silver have forced dozens of mines to close in the past decade. Through 1997 the spot price of silver hovered at a mere $5 an ounce. Moreover, the market for molybdenum has almost totally disappeared in the past decade, leaving the closed molybdenum mine north of Taos, New Mexico, an oozing pit visible from space.

The U.S. tax code contributes to the specula-

Mining by the Numbers
Since 1993

Price/acre to buy public land under the Mining Law	$5
Cost/cubic yard of sand for sandbox	$6
Transfers of public land to mining companies	32
Payments to U.S. treasury for these transfers	$17,000
Royalties paid to the U.S. for minerals removed from public land	none
Value of resources xfered to mining companies	$153 billion
Public land "sold" to mining co's under Mining Law	23,000,000 acres
# of operating open pit mines in 12 Western states	120
# of abandoned mines in 12 Western states	560,000
Miles of stream poisoned by mining	12,000
Cost/day to U.S. treasury to stabilize Summitville disaster	$40,000
Average size of open-pit mine	350 acres
Depth of open pit mine	1,200 feet
Height of Empire State Building	1,500 feet
Value of gold removed from average open pit mine	$380 million
Average life span of open pit mine	8 to 10 years

George Bush and
the $10 Billion Golden Prize

Prior to leaving the White House, George Bush announced he was not going to trade in on his time as President by jumping on to a lucrative position on the board of directors of major corporations. Then in the spring of 1994, Bush reversed himself and did just that. But the company he chose to join, Barrick Resources, might have been a surprise to many. After all, it was an obscure Canadian mining firm. Yet, this company had pulled off one of the most outlandish deals in modern times when it purchased from the federal government public land in Nevada harboring more than $10 billion worth of gold for only $10,000. President Bush helped make the deal possible, when his administration sped up the permitting process in order to beat an attempt by Congress to halt the sale of the land. Also sitting on Barrick's board are former Canadian Prime Minister Brian Mulroney and Washington lobbyist Vernon Jordon. Since joining Barrick, Bush has used his foreign policy clout to aid the company's plans to expand its operations in Indonesia.

---

tive and wasteful nature of the industry by granting mining companies a depletion allowance. This tax credit—valued at more than $1 billion a year—allows companies to deduct the value of minerals as they are mined, even if the minerals are located on lands owned by the federal government. Since mining companies can recoup many times over the cost of their initial investment, the depletion allowance acts as a tremendous incentive to mine as quickly and abusively as possible.

Gold Mining on the Increase

The one hardrock mineral that seems somewhat immune to this trend is gold, which has been booming since the 1980s. Gold production has increased tenfold in the last decade. The resurgence in gold mining

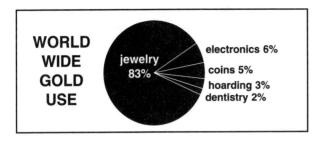

WORLD WIDE GOLD USE

jewelry 83%
electronics 6%
coins 5%
hoarding 3%
dentistry 2%

was sparked by the development of a new technology called cyanide heap leach mining that made it possible to cheaply extract gold from otherwise uneconomical lands. In this highly destructive and toxic method, giant holes are blasted into mountainsides, the rock is excavated, crushed, and drenched in a cyanide bath

An Occurence at Summitville

In the San Juan Mountains of southern Colorado lies one of modern mining's greatest disasters: Summitville. Over about a 10-year period a Canadian mining company called Galactic Resources removed some 300,000 ounces of gold worth more than $110 million dollars. Then the dam that was designed to hold back the cyanide used to leach the gold out of the crushed rock began to leak. It had been poorly and cheaply built. The toxic chemicals streamed into the Alamosa River at a rate of 3,000 gallons a minute, poisoning a 17-mile stretch which was heavily used by farms and ranches in the San Luis Valley. When the government increased the reclamation bond from $2 million to $7 million, Galactic Resources simply closed down, declared bankruptcy and left the United States. The mine, including 160 million gallons of cyanide, is now a Superfund site and the cleanup costs may exceed $150 million. The owner of Galactic Resources, Robert Freidlander, resurfaced a year later with a new company in South America, Golden Star Resources. In August of 1996, this firm spilled 700 million gallons of cyanide mining waste into a river in Guyana. Friedland's new company, Diamond Fields, is developing a copper mine in the Canadian Arctic.

┌─DISHONORABLE MENTION─┐

Mining Companies

ANGLO-AMERICAN CORPORATION is one of the world's biggest mining conglomerates (the U.S. subsidiary is Minorco). Formed in 1917 to fund diamond and gold mining operations in South Africa, it profited from cheap black labor in southern Africa and was a staunch defender of apartheid. It fired 60,000 striking black workers in 1987. A 1996 investigation recommended that the company be charged with homicide for deaths of 104 miners in a train wreck. Like other foreign corporations operating in the U.S., it pays only one percent of its revenues in taxes.

BARRICK RESOURCES, INC., is making a run toward becoming one of the world's biggest mining conglomerates with properties in Canada, South America, and Indonesia. It owns the most lucrative gold mine in the United States, the Goldstrike Mine in northern Nevada. Barrick was bruised in 1997 by its involvement in the Bre-X scandal, where it was a lead investor in the gold mine scam in Indonesia.

CYPRUS AMAX, one of the new titans of the mining indus-

that leaches flecks of gold from tons of rock. Homestake's new Ruby Mountain mine in Nevada, touted as a fabulous new find, will yield less than one-tenth of an ounce of gold per ton of rock!

Gold is far from an essential good. Some of the gold mined in the U.S. ends up back underground, bought by national governments and stored deep in the vaults of the Federal Reserve Bank in New York City. Increasingly, however, American gold and silver ends up overseas for processing in the trinket and jewelry shops of India and Pakistan. Strangely, the biggest importer of gold in the world is the tiny Arab sheikdom of Dubai, which imports 660 tons of gold every year. ☠

try, now controls mines in a dozen states, Chile, Peru, Australia, and Russia. Its large open pit mine on the Tohono O'Odham Indian Reservation in Arizona has been plagued by toxic run-off. It mines 76 million tons of coal a year, much of it high-sulfur coal from strip mines in West Virginia, Pennsylvania, and Kentucky. In 1997 Cyprus Amax was smacked with an $80 million fine for repeated violations of air and water standards at its Arizona copper mine.

ECHO BAY this is a Canadian firm operating three mines on public lands in the U.S. and one on native settlement land outside Yellowknife in northern Canada. Echo Bay's large McCoy mine property sprawls across 45,000 acres of Bureau of Land Management land in Nevada. In 1996 residents of Juneau, Alaska, fought back Echo Bay's plans to open a vast gold mine near the city using an experimental technique to bury its toxic mining waste called "submarine tailings disposal."

HOMESTAKE MINING, made its fortune from the giant Homestake mine in the Black Hills of South Dakota and now controls mines across the West containing over 50 million ounces of gold and 245 million ounces of silver. It is also engaged in the mining of off-shore sulfur deposits in the Gulf of Mexico. Homestake has left a trail of hazardous waste sites across the country, including lead contamination in Missouri, uranium at its plant in Grants, New Mexico, and the poisoning of Whitewood Creek in South Dakota.

FREEPORT McMORAN shed itself of its American gold holdings in 1990 to concentrate on its operations in Indonesia, where it owns the world's largest gold and copper mine, the Grasberg Mine. The company's activities in Indonesia have sparked criticism from international environmental groups and human rights organizations, who have accused Freeport of poisoning water supplies with arsenic mine wastes, destruction of tribal villages, and forced relocation of thousands of native Aumungme people. To help fend off international campaigns against the company, Freeport has loaded its board of directors with high-profile "fixers," such as Henry Kissinger.

NEWMONT MINING is the biggest and most aggressive gold company in the United States. Most of its production comes from the huge open-pit mine in Nevada's Carlin Trend. Newmont has also become a major player in Indonesia and the former Soviet republic of Uzbekistan. In 1995, it announced plans to develop a mammoth mine in the Alaskan wilderness.

Image on mining company t-shirt.

NORANDA is one of Canada's most powerful corporations. More than 40 percent of Noranda's stock is controlled by the Bronfman family, owners of Seagram's. Noranda developed the New World mine near Yellowstone Park and has a major stake in North America's richest gold reserve, Carlin Trend in Nevada. Its environmental record in South America has come under harsh international criticism.

PEGASUS GOLD operates the troubled Zortman-Landusky mine on lands that were on the Belknap Indian Reservation in Montana. Its executives have attacked the funders of environmental groups who are working with Native Americans to stop the mine. Pegasus's president sent a threatening letter to the Educational Foundation of America, saying "I hold the Foundation partially accountable for the damage being done to this company's operations and to its business reputation."

RIO TINTO PLC is the world's largest mining conglomerate. Its Mojave Desert mine alone produces half the world's boron. It owns the world's two largest copper mines, the Escondid in Chile and the Kennecott mine at Bingham Canyon in Utah, which in 1988 was listed by the EPA as producing more than 170 million pounds of toxic waste, making it the nation's fourth largest polluter.

James R. Moffett
CEO Freeport McMoRan Copper & Gold

SALARY
$41 million

EDUCATION:
University of Texas

NICKNAME:
JimBob

BUSINESS PROFILE:
Built McMoRan by combining oil drilling operation he started after school with Freeport.

BEST DEAL WHEELED:
Making $5.50 per second ($19,700 an hour), or more than 1000 times the average American worker.

ALAN POGUE

GROVES OF ACADEME:
Having his own endowed professor in his own building at University of Texas, Austin

QUOTABLE QUOTE:
"[It's] equivalent to me pissing in the Arafura Sea," commenting on the pollution from his company's mining operation in the Irian Jaya.

phelps dodge Corporation

ANNUAL SALES
$3.7 billion

HEADQUARTERS
Phoenix, Arizona

CEO/SALARY
Douglas Yearley
$1.35 million

PRODUCTS
• copper
• zinc
• gold & silver
• lead
• uranium

LOCATION OF MINES
• Arizona
• New Mexico
• Texas
• Montana

POLITICAL CONTRIBUTIONS
• $82,000
• South Africa
• Mexico
• China

ENVIRONMENTAL RAPSHEET
• Phelps Dodge is one of the world's largest producers of copper, much of which is exported to Korea and China.
• It is one of the largest consumers of water in the Southwest, drawing tens of millions of gallons a day from the Colorado River.
• The EPA has listed Phelps Dodge as being responsible for at least 37 toxic waste sites across the country.
• Its copper smelters and refineries in Arizona and Texas have been cited for numerous clean air violations.
• In 1996, the company was forced to spend $116 million in environmental remediation.

ASARCO *incorporated*

ANNUAL SALES
$2.6 billion

PRODUCTS
• copper
• lead
• zinc
• silver
• molybdenium

LOCATION OF MINES
• Idaho
• Arizona
• Montana

HEADQUARTERS
New York, NY

CEO/SALARY
Richard Osborne
$1.3 million

POLITICAL CONTRIBUTIONS
• $59,000

ENVIRONMENTAL RAPSHEET
• Asarco, created by Standard Oil tycoon Henry Rogers and the Guggenheims and one of world's largest copper companies, was rated the nation's top polluting company by the EPA in 1996.
• It has a vicious history of suppressing striking laborers.
• Until 1989 it was a leading producer of asbestos.
• Poisonous run-off from its mines in northern Idaho has prompted multi-million dollar suits by the federal government and local citizens, and faces millions in fines for improper disposal of mining waste in Montana, where it owns 49 percent of the notorious Berkeley Pit outside Butte.

Agriculture

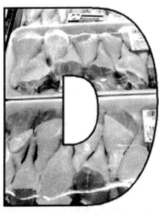

ESPITE THE MYTH OF THE small "family farmer," American agriculture has been dominated from the beginning by big business, starting with the British-financed railroads which first colonized the western plains, bringing immigrants from Europe to settle the land under land grants provided by Congress. The railroads divided up the land, dropped off the settlers, provided them with seeds, equipment and other supplies—always with a view to supplying their own developing markets. And in our modern highly mechanized agribusiness culture, the railroads remain big landholders who participate in the food business along with a handful of giant agribusiness companies.

Today the biggest single chunk of the food dollar goes for meat. Four companies—International

Beef Processors, ConAgra, Cargill, and National Beef—control 87 percent of beef production, far more than the concentration in 1919 when the government stepped in with the famous legislation to break up the beef packing cartel.

The largest single player in the food industry is Philip Morris, a company most often connected in the public mind with tobacco, but actually a large player in the overall food business. This firm alone gets 10 cents of every dollar spent on food. ConAgra gets 6 cents.

The concentration goes on: Tyson, Gold Kist, Perdue, and ConAgra control 55 percent of the poultry market. Four firms hold 73 percent of lamb. Four firms have about two-thirds of all flour and corn milling, as well as 76 percent of soybean processing and ethanol production, according to William D. Hefferman of the University of Missouri's Department of Rural Sociology.

Moreover, all of these companies are vertically integrated: controlling meat production from the

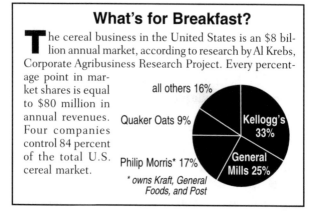

What's for Breakfast?

The cereal business in the United States is an $8 billion annual market, according to research by Al Krebs, Corporate Agribusiness Research Project. Every percentage point in market shares is equal to $80 million in annual revenues. Four companies control 84 percent of the total U.S. cereal market.

all others 16%

Quaker Oats 9%

Kellogg's 33%

Philip Morris* 17%

General Mills 25%

* owns Kraft, General Foods, and Post

animal's birth to the supermarket. Companies such as ConAgra and Cargill even raise their own grain for feed, while other big companies maintain contracts for grain with other huge agribusiness compa-

---

E. Coli Lobby

Only 43 percent of all meat products recalled by their manufacturers from 1990 to 1997 was actually recovered, with the rest—17 million pounds of contaminated meat—eaten by unsuspecting consumers, according to a 1995 study by the Center for Public Integrity. Meanwhile, in 1994, 1995, and 1997 Congress and the meatpackers opposed granting the Secretary of Agriculture authority to issue mandatory recalls of contaminated meat.

Over the last decade the food industry gave more than $41 million to the treasuries of Capitol Hill lawmakers, more than a third of it to members of the House and Senate Agriculture committees. Among the recipients: Agriculture Secretary Dan Glickman; majority and minority leaders in the Senate: Trent Lott and Tom Daschle; Speaker of the House and House minority leader: Newt Gingrich and Dick Gephardt and six past and present chairmen or ranking minority members of the Senate and House Agriculture committees.

One of the most effective lobbies ever seen in Washington, the meat industry has recruited federal lawmakers and congressional aides for influence peddling. Of 124 lobbyists whom the Center for Public Integrity identified as working for the meat industry in 1997, at least 28 previously worked on Capitol Hill.

In early 1997 the Clinton administration proposed having food processors themselves pay for government inspections of their meat, poultry, and egg products. The plan was denounced by members of Congress, including House Agriculture Committee chairman Bob Smith of Oregon as "unwise and unnecessary." The Center discovered Smith and his staff took more than 40 trips underwritten by food industry interests in 1996 and the first half of 1997.

All in all, the Center found: "During the escalating public health crisis of the past decade, the food industry has managed to kill every bill that has promised meaningful reform."

Feedlots

"Agricultural practices in the United States are estimated to contribute to the impairment of 60 percent of the nation's surveyed rivers and streams; 50 percent of the nation's surveyed lakes, ponds, and reservoirs; and 34 percent of the nation's surveyed estuaries. Feedlots alone, not including the potential runoff from farms using manure as fertilizer, are estimated to adversely impact 16 percent of the waters impaired by agricultural practices. Agricultural feeding operations have also been identified as substantial contributors to nutrients (e.g., nitrogen and phosphorous) in water bodies that have experienced severe anoxia (i.e., low levels of dissolved oxygen) or outbreaks of microbes, such as *Pfiesteria piscicida*."

EPA, *Strategy for Addressing Environmental and Public Health Impacts from Animal Feeding Operations*, March,1998

Major Sources of Impairment of Surface Water Resources in the United States

TYPE OF WATER BODY	IMPAIRED	MAJOR SOURCES OF IMPAIRMENT*
Rivers and Streams (17% of 3.5 million miles surveyed)	**36%**	Agriculture (60%) Municipal Point Sources (17%) Hydro./Habitat Mod. (17%)
Lakes, Ponds, and Reservoirs (42% of 41 million acres surveyed)	**37%**	Agriculture (50%) Municipal Point Sources (19%) Urban Runoff/Storm Sewer (18%) Unspecified Nonpoint Source (15%)
Estuaries (78% of 34,000 sq. miles surveyed)	**37%**	Urban Runoff/Storm Sewer (46%) Municipal Point Sources (39%) Agriculture (34%) Industrial Point Sources (27%)

* The percentage reflects the relative proportion of surface water affected by each major source of impairment. *Source:* National Water Quality Inventory: 1994 Report to Congress, *U.S. EPA, Office of Water, 1995.*

---

nies such as Archer-Daniels-Midland.

In farming, the big processing companies along with banks and insurance companies, call the tune. They finance farm mortgages, and provide the funds upfront for planting and harvesting crops. They are a hidden hand, determining the type and amount of crop by the conditions of their loans.

The top 10 states in total agricultural market value are California, Texas, Iowa, Kansas, Nebraska, Illinois, Minnesota, Florida, Wisconsin, and North

---

Farmland at Risk

When AFT analyzed the country's 181 geographic regions known as Major Land Resource Areas (MLRA), 70 percent had high quality farmland in the same areas where rapid development was occurring. The greatest loss of prime or unique farmland occurred in 20 MLRAs representing 7 percent of the land in the continental United States. Twenty-one percent of the prime or unique farmland conversion that took place occurred within these areas:

Sacramento and **San Joaquin Valleys** (central California)

Northern Piedmont (primarily parts of Maryland, New Jersey, Pennsylvania and Virginia)

Southern Wisconsin and **Northern Illinois Drift Plain** (parts of Illinois and Wisconsin)

Texas Blackland Prairie (eastern part of Texas)

Willamette and **Puget Sound Valleys** (parts of Oregon and Washington)

Florida Everglades and associated areas (southern tip of Florida)

Eastern Ohio Till Plain (primarily parts of Ohio)

Lower Rio Grande Plain (southern Texas)

Mid-Atlantic Coastal Plain (primarily parts of Delaware and Maryland)

New England and **Eastern New York Upland,** *Southern Part* (primarily parts of Connecticut, Massachusetts, New Hampshire, New Jersey, New York and Rhode Island)

Ontario Plain and **Finger Lakes Region** (western New York)

Nashville Basin (central Tennessee)

Central Snake River Plains (parts of Idaho)

Southwestern Michigan Fruit and Truck Belt (southwestern Michigan)

Central California Coastal Valleys (central coast of California)

Columbia Basin (primarily parts of Washington)

Imperial Valley (southern California)

Long Island-Cape Cod Coastal Lowland (parts of Massachusetts, New York and Rhode Island)

Connecticut Valley (primarily parts of Connecticut and Massachusetts)

Western Michigan Fruit and Truck Belt (parts of Michigan and Wisconsin)

Big Profits in Cereal

The U.S. cereal market is probably the most profitable sector of corporate agribusiness. The average annual return on equity (profitability) from 1991 to 1995 for the four largest cereal manufacturers was:

General Mills	65%
Quaker Oats	51%
Philip Morris	36%
Kellogg's	36%

The 1991-1995 average median for the food, beverage and tobacco processing industry was 15 percent, for all U.S. industry it was 13 percent, and for U.S. agriculture the 1991–1995 annual average was 2 percent.

"History shows that a one-time 10 percent drop in grain prices is associated with declines of 2.3 percent in the prices of foodstuffs/feedstuffs and declines of only about 1 percent in the prices of processed and wholesale foods. Effects on foodstuff/feedstuff prices would last six months, on average, compared with three months for the prices of processed and wholesale foods." (*Agricultural Outlook*, USDA, March 1993)

Al Krebs, Corporate Agribusiness Research Project

Carolina. Much of the potential threat to the United States production of fruits and vegetables is due to development pressures in California and Florida. Per acre, the New England states with their high-value crops dominate the top 10. Ranked by market value per acre of farmland, Delaware, Connecticut, Rhode Island, Massachusetts, New Jersey, California, North Carolina, Maryland, Pennsylvania, and Florida are the top 10 producing states. More and more, as the reports of the American Farm Land Trust make clear, prime agricultural land is moving from farm to urban development where the returns are higher. American Farmland Trust's analysis shows that between 1982 and 1992, every state lost some of its high quality farmland, prime or unique, to urban de-

Lawn Pesticides

Of the 36 pesticides most commonly used by Americans on their lawns, 32 have never been fully tested by the EPA. In 1987, Representative George Brown, a Democrat from California, declared, "the inability of the federal government . . . to give informed answers about the health and safety of currently registered pesticides is both a national disgrace and an economic disaster." It still is.

—Center for Public Integrity, 1998

---

velopment. Texas lost more prime and unique farmland than any other state (490,000 acres), accounting for 12 percent of the total loss in the United States. Other leading states with farmland lost to urban development were North Carolina, Ohio, Georgia, Louisiana, Florida, Illinois, Tennessee, Indiana, and California.

The highly mechanized farm operations that are left, especially those in beef, pork, and chicken, have become immense causes of pollution. The appear-

■ DIRTY MEAT ■

In 1993 four children in the Pacific Northwest died and 175 people were hospitalized after eating E. coli-contaminated hamburgers sold by Jack-in-the-Box. The tots' fate made headlines, but there was nothing unusual about the fatalities. Each year some 500 people in America die and more than 20,000 fall ill from dirty meat. Salmonella-contaminated chicken afflicts nearly two million people a year in the U.S., finishing off some 2,000 for good. One USDA

> "Eating processed chicken was like eating something that had been dunked in a toilet."

microbiologist said that eating processed chicken was like eating something that had been dunked in a toilet.

After the Jack-in-the-Box deaths, the Clinton administration rushed out new regulations but the new rules avoided dealing with the underlying causes of dirty meat: overcrowded feedlots, filthy slaughterhouses, and contaminated processing plants. The inspection rules negotiated with the companies allow the meat industry to do their own inspections and permit the companies to label their safety records "trade secrets," thereby shielding them from public review.

One of the main problems is concentration, which allows Big Meat to command great political influence, control prices, and dictate the means of production. Also, despite steady or higher meat prices for consumers, small ranchers and family farmers have gone under because their prices to the meat packers have plummeted as cattle production has concentrated in the big feedlots.

The same fierce concentration has struck the pork industry. In 1974 there were 750,000 hog farms across the country. Today there are 250,000, with most of them entirely dependent on the big hog-buying companies such as the North Carolina-based Murphy Farms.

The consolidation of the poultry industry—already far advanced 20 years ago—took another leap with the mass production of McDonald's Chicken McNuggets, accounting for 10 percent of all chickens grown each year in America.

These accelerating levels of concentration make dirty meat more likely as the big corporations push for "more efficient"—that is, cheaper—production methods, such as assembly-line food factories, where animals are reared in unsanitary and inhumane conditions. The average chicken pen now holds 20,000 birds. Hogs are raised in huge metal barns holding more than 1,000 pigs that stand on metal grates which allow their excrement to fall into water troughs. These wretched conditions are breeding grounds for the deadly bacteria that threaten human health.

---

ance of red tide pfiesteria, a lethal bacteria, first in a river in North Carolina near a pork feedlot and later in the southern reaches of the Chesapeake Bay around chicken processing operations, clearly illustrates this problem.

Agricultural pesticides are a growing source of chemical pollution. National use of pesticides have grown from about 540 million pounds in 1964 to 1100 million pounds in 1993. Agriculture accounts

The Top 10 Landowners

The 100 largest landowners in the U.S. (originally published in *Worth* magazine, February 1997) own more than 1 percent of the nation—a landmass the size of Kentucky. Two big businessmen—Ted Turner of CNN and Henry Singleton of the timber business together own 3 percent of New Mexico.

1 R.E. "Ted" Turner, Roswell, GA: 1.3 million acres in Montana, Nebraska, Florida, Georgia, South Carolina, and New Mexico (where Turner owns 1.15 million acres or 1.5 percent of the state).

2 Archie Aldis "Red" Emmerson, Anderson, CA: 1.2 million acres of forests in California.

3 Henry E. Singleton, Beverly Hills, CA: 1.15 million acres in California and New Mexico, mostly cattle ranches where he owns 1.4 percent of New Mexico.

4 Pingree Heirs, Bangor, ME: Pingree Associates and Seven Islands Land oversee 975,000 acres of timberlands in Maine and elsewhere.

5 King Ranch Heirs, Kingsville, TX: 860,000 acres in Texas, Florida and Kentucky devoted to agribusiness operations in cattle, farming, oil, and gas.

6 Huber Family, Rumson, NJ: 800,000 acres in Maine, Tennessee, Kentucky, Missouri, and West Virginia. J.M. Huber Corp. produces electronic and chemical products and owns timberlands.

7 Reed Family, Seattle, WA: 770,000 acres of forest lands held through Simpson Investment in Washington, Oregon, California.

8 Kenneth W. Ford, Roseburg, OR: 740,000 acres of timberlands in Oregon and California.

9 Lykes Family, Tampa, FL: 640,000 acres in Florida and Texas in cattle, citrus, and other agricultural products

10 Dolph Briscoe, Jr., Uvalde, TX: 600,000 acres in Texas devoted to cattle and agriculture.

---

for three quarters of all pesticide use. Pesticides have been detected in ground waters—used by half the nation for drinking—in more than 43 states. At least 143 pesticides and 21 transformation products, including compounds in every major chemical class, have been detected, according to a 1996 study by the U.S. Geological Survey. ☠

■ Bovine Growth Hormone ■

At the heart of the increasingly bitter controversy concerning the regulation of the nation's foods is the 10-year battle over recombinant bovine growth hormone—variously known as rBGH, BGH, rBST, or BST (for bovine somatatrophic hormone)—the genetically engineered hormone manufactured by Monsanto and sold under the brand name Posilac. It is claimed to increase the amount of milk a cow produces from 5 to 15 percent. Shortly after rBGH was introduced in 1994, about 5 percent of all cows in the United States are thought to have been injected with the drug (Monsanto cites 11 percent).

DISTURBING SIDE EFFECTS

Critics, however, insist rBGH has some very disturbing side effects. The drug can put the cow under considerable stress, causing her to develop mastitis, an udder inflammation that turns her milk into sour-smelling, pus-filled liquid. To correct this side effect, farmers must administer antibiotics. These cure the mastitis, but they stay in the milk and hence are passed on to anyone drinking it. The underlying concerns of scientists and consumers are that this sort of pollution in the milk supply will increase the general population's resistance to the beneficial effects of antibiotics and thus ultimately expose consumers to a wider range and intensity of disease.

> The drug can turn cows' milk into sour-smelling, pus-filled liquid; thus, antibiotics must be given to the cow.

In the drug's defense, the FDA insists that it inspects all milk and that the amount of antibiotics present does not exceed current safety standards. And although Monsanto warns that cows given rBGH may be more likely to contract mastitis, it downplays the significance on the condition.

Yet there are other problems. Some scientists argue that rBGH leads to an increase in milk of an insulin-like substance called IGF1, which has been linked to breast and colon cancer. Because of these questions, the European Economic Union placed a moratorium on its use until the turn of the century. A moratorium also applies in Canada.

On top of health worries, opponents point out that the increase in milk production exacerbates the existing milk surplus, driving prices down, and making it more—not less—difficult for the small and middle-sized dairy farmers to stay in business. And because the market for milk is already glutted, the always tenuous law of supply and demand does not apply in the dairy industry. Use of rBGH will not lower dairy prices, so it offers absolutely no consumer benefits to balance its reportedly harmful effects.

But for Monsanto, and for the rest of the chemical industry, rBGH is well worth fighting over because it's the forerunner of the industry's attempt to control and exploit the twenty-first-century food market. Milk from rBGH-injected cows is the first genetically engineered food to be FDA-approved for distribution nationwide, so its sale can be viewed as an important test case for the future: If the American people are willing to drink milk laced with genetically engineered hormones and drugs, they'll probably consume anything. Consumers Union estimated that rBGH could earn Monsanto $300 to $500 million annually in the U.S. and $1 billion each year worldwide.

THE BATTLE OVER LABELING

Consumer groups have been fighting to block rBGH by pressing state legislatures to pass labeling laws. These groups believe that if dairy products carried ingredient labels, it would be the kiss of death for genetically engineered foodstuffs. Monsanto has consistently fought labeling, arguing that it amounts to interference with interstate commerce.

Throughout the fights over the use of rBGH and the labeling of dairy products, the chemical industry has had the federal government on its side. Despite lingering health and economic concerns and a well-organized opposition, rBGH was approved in 1993 for general use by the FDA, which stated that the drug is safe and there is no significant difference between milk from treated and nontreated cows. The government has required no further studies, nor has it supported consumers' right to know whether or not they are consuming it.

> If Americans are willing to drink milk laced with genetically engineered hormones and drugs, they'll probably consume anything.

So in the end, it is not only the dairy farmers and their cows, but also the American public who have become unwitting subjects in this trial run on genetically engineered foods. "In essence," observes environmental writer Peter Montague, "FDA has given rBGH producers permission to conduct a large-scale experiment on the public, without a control group."

Methyl Bromide

In order to pass NAFTA, Clinton needed to secure the votes of 20-odd House members from Florida, and so promised to allow the continued use of methyl bromide—a controversial and highly toxic pesticide—on fruits and vegetables. Along with CFCs, methyl bromide is a key contributor in destroying the ozone layer above the earth. It is also the vital pest and post-harvest fumigant used by tomato farmers in Florida and strawberry farmers in California. It causes respiratory failure and has been

> If it were not considered a pesticide, it would be classified as toxic waste.

linked to more occupational deaths in California than all organophosphate insecticides combined. This lethal substance is also a neurotoxin and suspected human carcinogen. If it were not considered a pesticide, it would be classified as toxic waste.

Under the Montreal protocol of 1987, an international agreement designed to get rid of ozone-destroying chemicals, CFCs and methyl bromide were to be phased out by the year 2000. Furthermore, the Bush administration agreed to freeze methyl bromide production at 1991 levels.

PHASE OUT AGREEMENT REVERSED BY CLINTON

But it probably didn't hurt the pro-methyl bromide cause that the two companies that manufacture the pesticide (Ethyl and Great Lakes) have large plants in Arkansas and long-standing ties to Clinton. In a 1993 private letter to Florida growers, the Clinton administration promised that methyl bromide would not be restricted unless there were alternatives. The administration later claimed it never made such a promise, causing the Florida growers to accuse Clinton of a double cross.

In 1995, the Republican Right set out to scuttle all environmental regulations, making Clinton's double-crossing look like sage compromises. In this new atmosphere Clinton was able to advocate continued use of methyl bromide as part of a compromise to save environmental regulations across the board and in this way garner support from the environmental community in Washington. In 1995 EPA staffers phoned environmentalists in an effort to gain an agreement between environmentalists and growers on certain special uses that could basically exempt methyl bromide from the Clean Air Act ban.

At the same time Mary Nichols, the EPA's assistant commissioner for air and radiation, appeared before a House subcommittee saying, "[The administration] fully recognizes that there is no guarantee that acceptable alternatives will be available for all uses of methyl bromide prior to 2001. We believe that having a safety valve—allowing continued production for specified essential uses where no alternatives exist—is an important part of this process."

In September of 1995 the *Fresno Bee* reported that the California growers who met with Clinton heard him say he would support a delay of the chemical's phaseout plan if international competitors were still using it and no alternative existed.

FARMERS FORCED TO SOUTH OF BORDER

Because the farming which utilizes methyl bromide is one crop agriculture, more and more pesticides have to be used against the bugs. Sooner or later, tomatoes and strawberries, which currently are the most valuable crops per acre, will become so expensive to grow that they won't be worth the trouble.

It may well become cheaper, especially if the U.S. enacts tougher environmental rules, for the farmers to pursue large scale mono-agriculture in Latin America. Of course, it makes no difference to the atmosphere whether the ozone hole is depleted from emissions in the U.S. or Mexico.

When the farmers go south of the border, their U.S. lands become part of urban development, turning American farms into future venues for tract housing, which will wreak havoc with the environment in places like the great central valley of California. Florida farmers already have set up joint operations with Mexicans for tomato farming to take advantage of lower costs. Smaller farmers who can't afford to make the move will gradually go out of business.

> Sooner or later, tomatoes and strawberries will become so expensive to grow that they won't be worth the trouble.

Having set this migration in motion, Clinton blamed the effects of NAFTA on the Clean Air Act. The strictures of the environmental legislation, his administration contended, forced farms out of business or south of the U.S. He promised to lure the growers back, in part by alleviating the methyl bromide ban. At the same time, Clinton attacked environmentalists, saying that if they refused to compromise on methyl bromide, it would be their fault that farming leaves for Mexico.

Fish

During the past half century, the world's fish catch has been steadily rising, from 20 million tons in 1950 to 89 million in 1989. As a result, the high-value species of fish have been wiped out, and the fishing industry has turned to less commercially viable species. In part the rise of the modern fishing industry can be laid to the growth of huge transnational operations where big trawlers operating like factories travel the oceans for fish.

> Big trawlers operate like factories traveling the oceans for fish.

These operations are not the work of free enterprise, but the result of government subsidies which, according to a UN report far outstrip revenues: "[G]lobal annual expenditures on fishing amount to $124 billion—to catch just $70 billion worth of fish. Governments make up most of the $54 billion difference. . . ."

GOVERNMENT SUBSIDIES LEAD TO OVERFISHING

This has led to overproduction and overcapacity. Its effects have been severely felt in the developing nations of the southern part of the world, where nations dependent on the north have capitulated to foreign companies in developing fisheries to gain foreign exchange. The results are ironic: The world's finite fishing resources are decimated, and the fish, caught in third world waters, does little to alleviate hunger and improve diets of the local people, since it is almost always exported. And the local fishing industry loses out to the huge international trawlers that dominate the catch.

The U.S. has witnessed the virtual demise of its own once rich fisheries on both coasts. First in 1976 and again in 1987 the U.S. tried to regain control of its fisheries by establishing a 200-mile limit around its coasts and then by limiting foreign ownership of American vessels. But these measures have proved ineffective in that the largest fishing company in the northern Pacific, American Seafood Products, in 1998 was controlled by Norwegian interests. Not only have foreign interests continued to exercise powerful influence, but the organization of fisheries has led to economic concentration. Quotas for the size of a catch are set on the basis of historic record. This makes it difficult for new, small companies to gain a toehold in the business.

BAD GUY PROFILE:

Dwayne O. Andreas
Chairman and CEO, Archer Daniels Midland Co.

AGE:
77

EDUCATION:
attended Wheaton College

NICKNAME:
Senator Ethanol

BUSINESS PROFILE:
As "supermarket to the world," built ADM into the largest U.S. processor of farm commodities such as wheat, corn, and soybeans.

BEST DEAL WHEELED:
Single largest welfare recipient in America, costing American economy $40 billion from 1980-1995.

NOTABLE FACT:
"Tithing" to politicians including Thomas Dewey, Tip O'Neill, Richard Nixon, Hubert Humphrey, George Bush, Jimmy Carter, Michael Dukakis, Jack Kemp, Jesse Jackson, and Bob Dole

QUOTABLE QUOTES:
"There isn't one grain of anything in the world that is sold in a free market. Not one! The only place you see a free market is in the speeches of politicians. People who are not in the Midwest do not understand that this is a socialist country."
And, "I make the rules as I go along."

AP/WORLD WIDE PHOTOS

ANNUAL SALES
$72 billion

HEADQUARTERS
New York, NY

CEO/SALARY
Geoffrey C. Bible
$9.7 million

Philip Morris

POLITICAL CONTRIBUTIONS
• $2.4 million

PRODUCTS
• Marlboro cigarettes
• Kraft foods
• Oscar Meyer
• Jell-O

• Miller beer
• Post cereals
• Toblerone
• Tang
• Maxwell House coffee

LOBBY FEES
• $8 million

ENVIRONMENTAL RAPSHEET

• Embroiled with the other cigarette manufacturers in the smoking and health controversy, Philip Morris was accused in Minnesota of withholding documents about manipulating nicotine in Marlboro, the industry's leading cigarette, and other brands.

• According to papers released by its competitors, Philip Morris's "Secret of Marlboro" can be attributed to the controlled use of ammonia during the tobacco processing. A former Philip Morris research director, William Farone, told the FDA in 1996: "By controlling the ingredients that go into making reconstituted tobacco, the industry controls the chemical and physical properties . . . including its nicotine content." The company has refused to divulge trade secrets or open its manufacturing processes to public scrutiny.

• Sealed documents obtained by the Associated Press in the now settled ABC-TV libel suit accused Philip Morris of running a "tobacco extract factory" where employees measured the level of nicotine as the tobacco mixture was brewed.

• In 1997, subsidiaries (or former subsidiaries) of the company were involved in approximately 225 matters subjecting them to potential remediation costs under Superfund or otherwise.

  The company has been vigorously fighting these and other charges in Congress and in court.

ANNUAL SALES
$24 billion

Con Agra

HEADQUARTERS
Omaha, Nebraska

CEO/SALARY
Phillip B. Fletcher
$2.5 million

POLITICAL CONTRIBUTIONS
• $240,000

PRODUCTS
• Hunt's
• Healthy Choice
• Wesson
• LaChoy
• Chun King
• Knott's Berry Farm
• Armour
• Butterball
• Hebrew National
• Van Camp's
• Redenbacher's popcorn

LOBBY FEES
• $210,000

ENVIRONMENTAL RAPSHEET

• The company's Beatrice subsidiary faces environmental proceedings related to businesses it divested before it was bought by ConAgra. Beatrice is the potentially responsible party at 42 Superfund, proposed Superfund, or state-equivalent sites. Beatrice has paid or is in the process of paying its liability share at 40 of these sites.

• In 1996, the EPA filed an action in federal court in Idaho seeking civil monetary penalties for alleged violations of the Clean Water Act against a ConAgra beef packing plant.

• In 1997, the EPA filed an action against a subsidiary of the company which operates a pesticide formulation facility in Greeley, Colorado, seeking civil monetary penalties for violation of the Resource Conservation and Recovery Act.

• Also in 1997, the company agreed to pay $8 million to settle charges against its Peavey Co. unit in Indiana related to mishandling of grain at 12 grain elevators in the southeast region over a four-year period. The criminal plea agreement included one felony and three misdemeanors. The company also entered into a compliance agreement with the Dept. of Agriculture requiring further control systems at grain elevators.

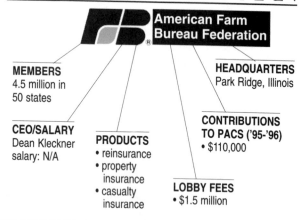

American Farm Bureau Federation

MEMBERS
4.5 million in
50 states

HEADQUARTERS
Park Ridge, Illinois

CEO/SALARY
Dean Kleckner
salary: N/A

PRODUCTS
• reinsurance
• property
  insurance
• casualty
  insurance

CONTRIBUTIONS TO PACS ('95-'96)
• $110,000

LOBBY FEES
• $1.5 million

ENVIRONMENTAL RAPSHEET
• As the voice of the nation's big mechanized farmers, the Farm Bureau scoffs at global warming as just so much "hot air"; takes credit for Senate resolution opposing Kyoto treaty.
• Opposes tighter pesticide restrictions on fruits and vegetables: "The[EPA] is now twisting the law in an all-out thrust to protect children and infants."
• Sneers at Endangered Species Act as "a failure."
• Fights legislation aimed at the rivers of animal shit pouring from chicken and pig factory farms that scientists believe are a cause of the deadly pfiesteria.
• Opposes strengthening wetlands legislation.
• Opposes expanding Clean Water legislation.
• Is against tighter federal controls on ozone and particulate matter.

NOTABLE FACT
Farm Bureau has investments in banks, mutual funds, financial trading companies, grain traders. Sixty-three Bureau-affiliated insurance companies earn more than $6.5 billion annually in net premiums, according to Defenders of Wildlife.

P A R T 2
Polluters

Garbage

HE NATION PRODUCES 210 million tons of municipal solid waste a year, or about four and a half pounds a person every day—62 percent of which goes into landfills, 15 percent to incinerators, and 23 percent is recovered—half of it paper and paperboard. During the 1980s, industrialized countries of the West sought to dispose of their wastes in Africa, and when those nations introduced laws to ban dumping, the focus shifted to the Caribbean. Turned away from that part of the world, the waste traders tried Central America and later the Middle East. Laws by individual developing nations, backed up by the Basel convention which bans dumping by the industrial nations in the Third World, have helped to slow the waste traffic. But it still continues, often under the guise of recycling, mostly to

Asia. There the main traffic is in lead acid batteries, dust from pollution control devices (lead and cadmium), and plastics.

PLASTICS "RECYCLING"

The program of so-called plastics recycling sends tons of plastic soft drink and other bottles and packaging to third world countries. Some of the used plas-

Who Will Take Our Poisons:

Faced with what to do with 15,000 tons of incinerator ash in the mid-1980s, Philadelphia tried to dump it in Ohio and the Carolinas. Then in 1986 Joseph Paulino & Sons, a carting concern, took over a $6 million contract to "properly dispose" of the ash, containing lead, cadmium, barium, arsenic, mercury, dioxin, and cyanide. Paolino contracted out to

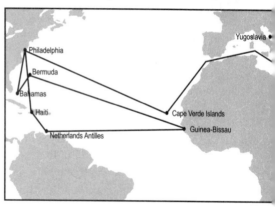

After starting in Philadelphia, the Khian Sea is rejected by the Bahamas, Dominican Republic, Honduras, Bermuda, Guinea-Bissau, Netherlands Antilles. In January 1988 it dumps 5,000 tons in Haiti but steals away in the night despite government demands to reload the ash. After returning to Philadelphia in March, it leaves for the Cape Verde islands against Coast Guard orders, then to Europe, reaching Yugoslavia in July, and changes

tic is made over into fiber for second-rate products, flip-flop shoes, and kitchen utensils for developing countries. But more than one-third is too dirty to recycle and it is dumped. Greenpeace researchers traced supposedly recycled plastic bottles from New York and California to Madras, India, where instead of being recycled, they are stacked in big piles. Ironi-

The Voyage of the Khian Sea

Amalgamated Shipping of the Bahamas to transport the ash. Amalgamated then chartered the cargo ship Khian Sea, with the help of a firm called Coastal Carriers. In August, 1986 the Khian Sea left Philadelphia with the ash for what was the beginning of a two-year journey to countries on five continents, each one of which rejected its load.

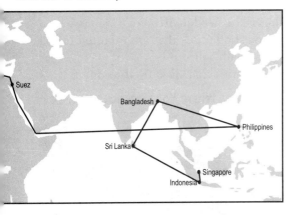

its name to Felicia, heads for Suez, where it claims its next port of call is the Philippines, tries to dock unsuccessfully in Bangladesh, Sri Lanka, and Indonesia. Finally, in November 1988, Felicia appears off Singapore with a new name, Pelicano, and an empty hold. In 1998, the Haitian government and Greepeace activists continue to campaign to get the ash returned from Haiti to the U.S.

From Garbage to Toxic Fertilizer

While outright dumping of toxic wastes from the industrialized world has been cut back with the Basel treaty, the practice still goes on. In 1997 the *Seattle Times* revealed how Exeter Energy Co., the largest rubber incinerator in the world, burns millions of used tires at its Sterling, Connecticut facility, then sells the ash to Bay Zinc, a firm based in central Washington, which turns it into fertilizer with a heavy zinc content for plant food (zinc is a bonding agent used in the manufacture of tires). Unfortunately, the fertilizer also contains cadmium and lead which comes from steel belts in the tires. This fertilizer is then sold to gardeners through hardware stores, employed by large farmers in the Great Plains, and is used as animal feed. The fertilizer has been distributed in 10 states (California, Colorado, Idaho, Kansas, Nebraska, North Dakota, Montana, Oregon, Washington, and Wyoming), as well as Canada, Mexico, and Australia.

cally Madras is the headquarters for a factory which makes new plastic bottles that are exported to the U.S. and filled with soft drinks.

Other countries that have tried to dump their wastes in Third World countries have all been forced by international reprisals and the weight of popular opinion to bring it back home. Italy has retrieved toxic waste from Lebanon and Nigeria; Ger-

Where Your Plastic Bottles Go

ANN LEONARD

Plastic recycling dump outside of Madras, India.

many from Albania and Romania; South Korea from China. But not the United States. Lenient regulations here require only that a company notify the EPA before shipping hazardous waste. If the company is caught vio-

> More than one-third of "recycled" plastic is too dirty to recycle and it is dumped.

lating foreign laws, the U.S. is not likely to prosecute. The United States itself continues a trade in waste with Canada, much of it going from the U.S. into a large landfill outside Montreal. Wastes from Canada are sent to the U.S. for recycling in incinerators. In the U.S., hazardous waste—some of it containing heavy metals—can be burned and then made into fertilizer which is used in growing plants

Alaska's Subartic Garbage Dump

When successive governments aren't trying to find ways to rip off Alaska's timber, minerals, oil, and other natural resources, they view the place as a "sub-arctic junkyard." In addition to nuclear testing, Alaska was a test site for nerve gas and germ warfare agents too deadly to experiment with elsewhere. At the secret Gerstle River test site at the 1,200-square-mile Fort Greely Military Reserve in Interior Alaska, mustard gas and nerve gas were packed into rockets and fired into nearby spruce forests, according to *Firecracker Boys* by Dan O'Neill. Not far away, the army tested bacterial disease agents (tularemia or rabbit fever) at Delta Creek in the open air. In one case the Army lost hundreds of rockets loaded with nerve gas when they sank through the ice on a frozen lake. A commander eventually followed up on rumors, pumped out the lake, and found 200 rockets, some of which had been leaking nerve gas into the lake bed. In 1970 the Army undertook a cleanup of the Gerstle River test site, pulling together four million pounds of chemical munitions, gas masks, contaminated clothing and equipment in two mounds and covering them with dirt.

and for animal feed.

The World Bank has run an ambitious program aimed at exporting medical waste burning incinerators to the third world that may well spew dioxin and other toxic pollutants into the atmosphere. And the U.S. actually maintains a project, organized through the Agency for International Development, to find markets for American technology in third world nations that help to hasten the export of pollution.

**Hospital Incineration:
The Literature**

MediBurn
PORTABLE MEDICAL WASTE THERMAL OXIDIZER

Within the U.S. the garbage industry continues to be transformed from a decentralized local industry with thousands of small companies into a national industry dominated by fewer big firms. Supreme Court decisions in the early 1990s essentially allow these firms to transport garbage from one place to another without interference of local laws. A turning point for the business occurred in New York City,

**Hospital Incineration:
The Practice**

ANN LEONARD

Burning medical wastes in a Delhi, India, hospital.

Oilfield Waste Dump

Grand Bois, a small Louisiana town on the Gulf once known for its good fishing and Cajun food, is now known for the putrid stench that permeates the air and the purplish fog that drapes the town on many summer days.

Increasingly, the residents of Grand Bois, many of whom are American Indians, have complained of burning eyes, respiratory problems, and severe headaches. There also has been an ominous spike in cancer rates. Residents point to a large oil

> Oilfield waste is larded with some of the most toxic compounds known, including benzene, hydrochloric acid, and lead.

field waste disposal dump located only a few yards from town as the culprit.

The Grand Bois dump is one of the largest in the South. Its two dozen open pits receive millions of gallons of oil waste from Exxon and other big companies *every week*. The waste is allowed to settle for months in the pits before it is injected into underground wells. Oilfield waste is larded with some of the most toxic compounds known, including benzene, hydrochloric acid, lead, and chlorine.

Off-shore oil waste is considered a hazardous waste and its disposal is strictly regulated by the EPA under the Resource Recovery and Conservation Act. But through a quirk of politics that tells much of the lobbying might of the oil industry, oil field waste generated from onshore wells is not considered toxic and its disposal is entirely left up to state laws. All Louisiana requires is that oil waste dumps be located no closer than 500 feet from homes. But even this law is not en-

> *The residents:* Burning eyes, respiratory problems, severe headaches.
> *The company:* It's probably tree pollen, household cleaners, or psychosomatic.

forced in Grand Bois, where several homes are perched on the very edge of the pits. This feeble environmental standard has made Grand Bois a dumping ground for oil waste from sites throughout the South.

The Congressional Record for the debate on the Resource Recovery and Conservation Act, the nation's main hazardous waste law, reveals the reason for this double standard: "The regulation of oil field waste would cause a severe economic impact on the industry and oil and gas production in the U.S." The exemption was moved through Congress with the help of three heavy hitters in the Louisiana delegation, former Sen. Bennett Johnston, Sen. John Breaux, and Rep. Billy Tauzin.

PR flacks from US Liquids, the company that manages the dump, contend that the residents' symptoms are more likely the result of exposure to household cleaners or tree pollen. Another US Liquids official said the illnesses were probably psychosomatic. Both US Liquids and Exxon have gone to court in an attempt to keep journalists from reviewing records on the Grand Bois dump, claiming that such reporting might "poison public opinion."

But the sleight of hand was effectively demolished when a toxicologist from Louisiana State University released a study showing that more than 20 of the town's children were suffering from lead poisoning. "It's scary to know that our government would allow this to go on," says Grand Bois resident Danny Friloux. "And the more we dig, the scarier it gets."

which with seven million inhabitants has the densest and most lucrative garbage business in the nation. For years that business has been dominated by the Mob, but under pressure from the city's district attorney and with the assistance of one big company, BFI, the garbage business was successfully prosecuted under Mayor Rudolph Giuliani, and the business was opened to competition with BFI and with Waste Management coming into the market. But even as the city opened its garbage industry to competition, the industry became more concentrated as two top players in New York—Waste Management and USA Waste—merged to form the world's largest garbage company.

New York had sent much of its trash to a landfill in its Staten Island borough, but as that big landfill made plans to close, the city began to pay haulers to cart New York garbage by truck, rail, and barge as far away as Virginia, where landfills became a controversial but lucrative business. Pennsylvania became the largest garbage importing state in the country, and most New York area garbage was destined for landfills there. But there were plans to export garbage further afield, with one company proposing to haul trash from the New York metropolitan area to as far away as Utah. One consortium offered to ship garbage to a power plant off the coast of Africa where it could become a source of fuel for electricity. And a Chinese trading company made inquiries for long term export of trash to South China and other countries in Asia where it could be mixed with chemicals and turned into road building materials.

> Superfund progress proceeds at a snail's pace, with money for the cleanup running out and Congress unable or unwilling to work out an efficient program.

The new garbage business unfolds against a landscape pitted with over 1200 Superfund dumps filled with toxic wastes that under the law are supposed to be cleaned up by the companies that caused them. But Superfund progress proceeds at a snail's pace, with money for the cleanup running out and Congress unable or unwilling to work out an efficient program. ☠

William Ruckelshaus
Chairman, BFI

AGE:
66

EDUCATION:
Princeton

NICKNAME:
"Mr. Clean"

BACKGROUND:
First director of EPA in 1970s, returning in 1983 to extricate agency from Rita Lavelle scandal to run the agency in 1983.

BIGGEST ACCOMPLISHMENT:
Resigned as Richard Nixon's deputy attorney general rather than execute an order to fire Watergate special prosecutor Archibald Cox. Ruckelshaus has played a key role in organizing the evolving national garbage industry dominated by a handful of giant companies. He formed an alliance with New York City's District Attorney Robert Morgenthau in 1993 to break the stranglehold of the Mafia on the city's garbage business. As a result the mob was banished, and New York's lucrative garbage business was opened to competition. But where the mob maintained one form of monopoly, the free market competition sponsored by Ruckelshaus and Morgenthau quickly showed signs of being transformed into its own monopoly where two or three big waste haulers control a much larger national market.

QUOTE:
"All it takes is one guy to do something dumb."

BAD GUY PROFILE:

WM

WASTE MANAGEMENT, INC.

ANNUAL SALES
$9.2 billion, WMI
$2.6 billion, USA Waste

CEO/SALARY
John Drury
$1.2 million

PRODUCTS
• garbage hauling
• recycling
• running landfills
• managing radioactive wastes

HEADQUARTERS
Houston, TX

POLITICAL CONTRIBUTIONS
• $440,000 WMI
• $23,000 USA Waste

LOBBYING
• $760,000 WMI
• $100,000 USA Waste

ENVIRONMENTAL RAPSHEET

The following report by the Ventura County, CA, sheriff's department provides a rough record of Waste Management from its founding in *1970 to 1991*:

• **Criminal violations**, 10; states involved, 5; total fines and penalties, $ 5 million.

• **Antitrust civil cases**, 23; states involved, 23; penalties, $23 million.

• **Environmental civil cases**, 22; states, 12; total fines and costs, $5 million.

• **Administrative cases**, 87; states involved, 13; fines and penalties, $3 million.

• **Chemical Waste Management**, a subsidiary of Waste Management, had the following judicial and administrative environmental actions: actions 81; states involved, 12; fines and penalties, $15 million.

• **Total fines and penalties** of the company for this period (1970-1991) is at least $52 million.

Since 1991, the Environmental Background Information Center in State College, PA, added these:

• December, 1991: Chemical Waste Management was fined $3.3 million for violations at its facility in Sauget, IL.

• October 15, 1992: Chemical Waste pled guilty and paid a record $11.6 million fine for six violations of environmental laws at a superfund.

Waste Management, Inc.

• In December 1996, a federal judge in Tennessee issued an opinion and court order fining Waste Management nearly $100 million, stating that the officers in Chem Waste Management had engaged in a fraudulent scheme to "cheat [the] plaintiffs out of money." The judge added," What is troubling about this case is that fraud, misrepresentation and dishonesty apparently became part of the operating culture of the Defendant corporation . . . There was no reason for Defendant to undertake such conduct other than greed."

• The federal government has cited USA Waste as the company responsible for cleaning up six Superfund sites, and the Justice Department has advised a Kentucky subsidiary that it is the target of an investigation relating to violations of the Clean Water Act.

OTHER POINTS OF INTEREST

• This company is an amalgam of Waste Management, Inc., which floundered in its bid to become a global trash giant, and the much smaller—but aggressive—USA Waste Services. The new firm is the largest garbage company in the U.S., hauling the garbage of 13 million residential, commercial, and industrial customers.

• The new Waste Management controls about 22 percent of the North American waste business. The company's international efforts are focused on Europe. George Soros, the international trader and philanthropist, owns 5 percent of the company.

• Founded in 1968 with the merger of waste disposal firms operating in Florida owned by H. Wayne Huizenga and companies in Chicago owned by Dean Buntrock, Waste Management was the world's largest garbage company. Over time the company gained a notorious reputation summed up by the statement of a city attorney in Indiana who declared that the state *"would have to grant a permit to Satan before they could grant a permit to this outfit."*

• USA Waste Services was founded in 1987, hauling garbage in Oklahoma. When John Drury, former president of Browning-Ferris, took over in 1994, the company grew dramatically with a series of acquisitions.

Nuclear

HERE IS LITTLE DOUBT but that the fossil fuels, on which the world's economies depend, will one day be exhausted. During the 1920s and again in the 1970s there were dire predictions of oil, gas, and even coal resources running out. These predictions turned out to be inaccurate, but they provided a backdrop for a debate on suitable alternatives—solar power, wind energy, and most of all, nuclear power.

Nuclear power is the direct outgrowth of the military-industrial complex and the Manhattan Project, which was a race by the U.S. to build the atomic bombs that destroyed the Japanese cities of Hiroshima and Nagasaki. At the war's end the bomb was miraculously transformed from an instrument of evil into a life-giving force. Through the valiant PR efforts of the Eisenhower administration, the atom bomb became the source of Atoms for Peace, electricity "too cheap to meter," nuclear cargo ships and planes, nuclear-propelled rockets, nuclear-sterilized sewage treatment, irradiated foods, and cures for cancer. Project Plowshare promised to rechannel rivers, move mountains, dig harbors and canals with nuclear explosions. The hazards of radiation and

AP/WIDE WORLD PHOTOS

"It's fun for the kids, and my wife is delighted to get away from the house for awhile."
—*James Schlesinger, AEC chairman in 1971 during his family's visit to Amchitka to observe underground tests.*

problems of disposing of nuclear wastes were swept aside in celebration of imagined productive uses of the bomb. And as recently as the 1970s oil crisis, nuclear power was seen as the answer to the Arab oil embargo.

> Nuclear power is a direct outgrowth of the race to build nuclear weapons.

An Outpouring of Protests

In the U.S. nuclear power was poised to become a major factor in electrical production during the 1970s when the accident at the Three Mile Island nuclear plant in Pennsylvania led to an outpouring

■ Criminal Activity by Rockwell ■

The Department of Energy ("DOE"), its contractors—Rockwell International, Inc, ("Rockwell"), EG&G, Inc. ("EG&G"), and many of their respective employees have engaged in an on-going criminal enterprise at the Rocky Flats Plant ("the Plant"), which has violated Federal environmental laws. This criminal enterprise continues to operate today at the Rocky Flats Plant, and it promises to continue operating into the future unless our Government, its contractors, and their respective employees are made subject to the law.

> Excerpts from a 1992
> Colorado Federal Grand
> Jury Report

When agents of the Federal Bureau of Investigation ("FBI") and the Environmental Protection Agency ("EPA") raided the Plant on June 6, 1989, they found compelling evidence that hazardous wastes and radioactive mixed wastes had been illegally stored, treated, and disposed of ("STD") at the Plant in violation of the Resource Conservation and Recovery Act ("RSCA"). These agents also discovered violations of the Clean Water Act and other environmental statutes through a variety of continuing acts, including the illegal discharge of pollutants, hazardous materials, and radioactive matter into the Platte River, Woman Creek, Walnut Creek, and the drinking water supplies for the Cities of Broomfield and Westminster, Colorado. These agents also uncovered a culture of criminal misconduct, which used illegal means to achieve corporate bonuses.

During the more than two and one-half years since the FBI raid, little has changed at the Rocky Flats Plant. DOE and EG&G employees continue to violate many Federal environmental laws at the Rocky Flats Plant. The continuing and pervasive nature of these criminal acts forms a pattern of behavior, which threatens to continue for an indefinite period of time into the future.

For 40 years, Federal, Colorado, and local regulators and elected officials have been unable to make DOE and the corporate operators of the Plant obey the law. Indeed, the Plant has been and continues to be operated by government and corporate employees, who have placed themselves above the law and who have hidden their illegal conduct behind the public's trust by engaging in a continuing campaign of distraction, deception, and dishonesty.

The ongoing nature of the criminal enterprise at the Rocky Flats Plant has prompted this Grand Jury to take three actions. First, the Grand Jury has approved indictments against certain current and former Federal employees, corporate employees, and corporations. Second, the Grand Jury has made presentments to this Court of evidence of criminal conduct by certain corporations and persons. Third, this Grand Jury strongly recommends that the Rocky Flats Plant be closed as the only means to stop the continuing nature of these criminal acts.

Colorado Federal District Court Report of the
Federal District Special Grand Jury 89-2, January 24, 1992

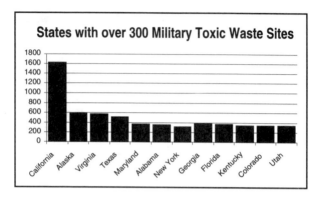

States with over 300 Military Toxic Waste Sites

of protests, causing President Jimmy Carter to put the brake on nuclear development. What killed nuclear energy then—at least over the near term—was the increasing flood of fossil fuel energy caused in part by deregulation and consequent rising prices. As the cost of fossil fuel energy, especially coal, remained low, the costs of nuclear power remained high by comparison.

The Rebirth of Nuclear Power

Today nuclear power may be headed for a partial rebirth. Research scientists believe they have developed a much safer sort of power system in the light water reactor. And probably most importantly, the international debate over global

> The Legacy: Bankrupt nuclear systems littering the nation.

warming has once again opened the door to a debate over nuclear power as a supposed clean energy source.

But the legacy of nuclear power is an ominous one, with bankrupt nuclear systems littering the nation from Washington state's public power system to the Long Island Lighting Company's white elephant at Shoreham. At Hanford, the most dangerous and polluted nuclear weapons site in the country, 55 million gallons of high-level wastes are stored in 177 underground tanks. According to the Department of Energy, 68 of them have already leaked. Electrical deregulation has added to the industry's woes, with Commonwealth Edison, the nation's largest atomic utility, announcing retirement of two of its 12 nuclear generating plants because they are too expensive.

Nuclear power accounted for about 20 percent of the nation's electricity output in 1997, down slightly from 22 percent in 1996. Analysts anticipate the overall share of nuclear power to decline steadily in the next two decades because no new plants are under construction in the U.S. ☠

▬▬▬ **Mobile Chernobyl** ▬▬▬

Nevada is one of the few states never to construct a nuclear power reactor. But now it is looking ever more certain that the "silver state" will become the graveyard of the nation's nuclear waste. A bill now winding its way through Congress mandates that lands at the Nevada Test Site will become the temporary parking lot for 95 percent of the radioactive waste generated by the

> Nuclear power waste to be shipped to Nevada from across the country for 30 years.

nation's 109 commercial nuclear reactor sites. The waste will accumulate at the temporary storage site 100 miles north of Las Vegas until being entombed within vaults deep inside nearby Yucca Mountain, the site on traditional Shoshone lands eyed by the nuclear industry as the final resting place for the nation's high-level nuclear waste.

At least that's the plan. Yucca Mountain is far from a sure

or safe bet. For one thing, geologists say the site leaks pose a real threat of nuclear waste hemorrhaging into groundwater. For another, it's on unstable terrain. This area of Nevada has been rocked by more than 650 earthquakes in the past 20 years. Even

> The Yucca Mountain site is earthquake prone and riddled with leaks.

so, if the nuclear industry's men in Washington are able to open a temporary storage site (prohibited by current law), the fate of the Yucca Mountain repository will probably be sealed as well, regardless of the economic or environmental costs.

The entire scheme has become known as the "mobile Chernobyl" plan. It calls for more than 30 years of continuous shipping by train and truck of 60,000 casks filled with irradiated reactor fuel, containing uranium, plutonium, strontium-90, cobalt-60, and cesium-137. A single rail cask harbors nearly 200 times as much cesium as was released by the Hiroshima atomic bomb. One study says that more than 300 "accidents" involving the shipment of this high-level nuclear waste can be expected. There is enough plutonium-239 in the waste stream to cause 1.5 million cancers.

The $4 billion plan's leading congressional advocate, Sen. Larry Craig (R-ID), is also its biggest political liability. Craig, one of the "singing Senators," has referred to the Yucca Mountain, lands long claimed as sacred by the western Shoshone, as "a desert wasteland."

But Craig's bumbling style is more than compensated for by the man the nuclear industry has tapped as its chief lobbyist, James Curtiss. Curtiss is now a partner in the high-powered DC lobby shop Winston & Strawn. Curtiss, who learned the trade as a member of the Nuclear Regulatory Commission during the Bush

> Over 300 "accidents" involving high-level nuclear waste are to be expected.

era, has built a powerful bipartisan coalition in the Congress, under the slogan that "one site is better than 100." Curtiss also has tried to pressure members of Congress by saying the federal government is contractually obligated to take possession of the commercial nuclear waste by the year 2008, or pay the companies billions in compensation.

Despite repeated declarations about the impeccable safety

of nuclear power, the nuke-laden utilities are getting nervous. For decades radioactive waste has been piling up on their property and with it billions of dollars in potential liability for leaks, accidents and radiation-induced cancers that the companies' own scientists and accountants tell them are inevitable. (One industry study claims that the nuclear industry may be facing as much as $56 billion in potential liabilities, unless it can unload the waste on the federal government.) Call it the nuclear debt. There are now more than 35,000 metric tons of radioactive waste from nuclear reactors, a toxic stockpile that is increasing by five tons a day. Scientists estimate that this glowing mountain of waste will take about four billion years to decay to "harmless" condition.

The Silent Warriors of the Cold War

That's what Michael Begay calls the men who worked the uranium mines during the 1950s, 60s, and 70s. For decades the mining of uranium was controlled by two companies, Kerr-McGee and Gulf Oil. With the aid of the Atomic Energy Commission, the companies recruited young Navajo and Hopi men to work in their uranium mines. The men were never

> Young Navajo and Hopi Recruited to Work in Uranium Mines

warned of any possible health risk and were never given any protective clothing or gear, even though both the companies and the government knew uranium to be a carcinogen.

After the passing of the Cold War and the decline of the nuclear power industry, the mining of uranium in the United States has slowed considerably. But the toxic legacy remains. Many of the Navajo miners have now contracted a range of diseases, including cancer. Yet, few have received any compensation. Uranium tailings from the old mine sites are lifted by the winds and blown across the Southwest. Then in 1979 a containment dam at the United Nuclear mine in New Mexico broke open, sending 90 million gallons of radioactive mine waste pouring into the Rio Puerca. Some of the land was covered with a thin coating of top soil and developed into public housing projects for impoverished Indians.

■ Aleutian Islands ■

Amchitka, a small island in the Aleutian island chain 1,300 miles southwest of Anchorage, is a wildlife refuge. It provides a roosting place for eagles, falcons, many migratory birds, as well as seals and sea lions. But it also had a long history of abuse by the United States. During World War II, it was the staging point for American attacks on the Japanese, who had taken two other Aleutian islands. Fifteen thousand troops were stationed

> **Alaskan Wildlife Refuge Turned into Military Dump**

there. When they left after the war, Amchitka was turned into a garbage dump.

In 1949, the U.S. military scuttled a World War II freighter off Amchitka filled with six millions tons of unexploded munitions, according to Dan O'Neill. Elsewhere along the Aleutian Island chain, the military dumped containers of mustard and blister gas, while leaving the rest of their war machine infrastructure—telegraph poles, docks, Quonset huts—to rust and decay.

Alaska as Nuclear Bomb Test Site

In 1951 the Atomic Energy Commission hit upon the idea of creating a huge harbor in Alaska by exploding an atom bomb. While both scientists and politicians warned against the plan, the AEC later launched a series of underground

> The final test in 1971 was by far the largest underground test ever carried out by the U.S., and was considered to be too large to be safely conducted in Nevada.

nuclear tests on Amchitka. (In fact, in 1966 the state's then governor Walter Hickel eagerly volunteered Alaska as a test site, offering the North Slope up to the AEC: "I would appreciate your opinion on the potential and possible use of Arctic Alaska as an atomic testing site," he wrote.) As the bombs got bigger, the Aleutian Islands seemed a good replacement for the Nevada test site, limited as it was by the growth of towns in the southwest.

Beginning in 1965 three nuclear tests were conducted on Amchitka. The final Cannikin test in 1971 was by far the largest underground test ever carried out by the U.S., and was considered to be too large to be safely conducted in Nevada.

At the time the proposed test was the center of intense controversy, with then Senator Mike Gravel and Congresswoman Patsy Mink, seeking legislation to ban it. When Congress refused, Gravel and others went to court. Protests poured in from around the world, with Japan's Emperor Hirohito and Canada's prime minister Pierre Trudeau joining in. But President Nixon stood firm, and the Supreme Court, over the vigorous dissent of William O. Douglas, let the test go forward. Justice Douglas warned, "the judgement of the Chairman of the Council on Environmental Quality is that it is likely, if not probable, that within 10 years of Cannikin, radioactive water of concentrations perhaps 100,000 times permitted maximums will reach the sea near Amchitka." By 1972 the AEC received reports of radioactive leakage into the atmosphere from the test site. The commission hid them from the public along with subsequent reports. Finally, in the summer of 1996 a Greenpeace expedition monitored samples that disclosed detectable levels of radioactive plutonium and americium in mosses and algae on the island.

> In 1972 the AEC hid reports of radioactive leakage from the public.

The Aleutians straddle the Bering Sea to the north and the Pacific to the south. The Bering Sea provides sole and perch to the U.S. market. But by far its biggest prize is pollock—with a catch worth $1 billion—which provides 60 percent of all fish caught in the U.S. and is used in fast food chain fish sandwiches. The Bering catch is dominated by two companies: Norwegian-controlled American Seafood and Tyson Seafood, an offshoot of the Arkansas poultry giant. A spokesman for American Seafood dismissed the report as "misleading," adding, "In my 10 years in the industry, I have never once heard of finding radiation in fish."

Military Dump Sites

Twelve states, including the most populous—California, New York, Texas, and Florida—are the centers of highly concentrated military and nuclear weapons toxic waste sites. California leads the nation with over 1600 different sites. According to the *New York Times*, "Sixty million Americans, almost a quarter of the population, live within 50 miles of military-related nuclear waste storage sites." Almost every U.S. military facility works with hazardous materials and generates toxic waste through activities such as the production, testing, cleaning and use of weapons, explosives and rocket fuels, vehicles, aircraft, and electronic equipment. Substances like PCBs, dioxin, heavy metals, and cyanides are emitted directly into the air, soil, and ground water.

> Sixty million people live within 50 miles of military-related nuclear waste storage sites.

According to a detailed report by the Physicians for Social Responsibility and the Military Toxics Project in May 1993, some sites, such as the Rocky Mountain Arsenal in Denver, are so polluted and clean up costs are so high that they may end up declared as "national sacrifice zones," leaving them fenced off for future generations to deal with. The Department of Defense has thus far identified over 11,000 polluted sites at 900 facilities on land they own. The Pentagon reports cleanup at fewer than 400 of the sites.

The DOE, which manages 14 major nuclear weapons facilities in 24 states, has built 60,000 nuclear weapons. According to the Office of Technology Assessment, deadly radioactivity and toxins have filtered beyond most of these sites into the surrounding air, groundwater, and streams. An estimated 385,000 cubic meters of "high-level" and 2.5 million cubic meters of "low-level" radioactive wastes are lying in "interim" storage in leaking tanks, drums, and trenches. Wastes from the Hanford, Washington facility alone would cover an area the size of Manhattan with a lake 40 feet deep. The Energy Department's own Advisory Committee on Nuclear Facility Safety has found that "the DOE has not adopted a cleanup policy with specific, clear objectives. . . . [This plan] appears to be scientific and unbiased, but in fact it is not. Because there is a lack of supporting data and analysis, the system can be manipulated at site level. There is only the illusion of scientific certainty and objectivity."

On the Road with Strontium 90

To solve the problem of what to do with nuclear wastes, the Department of Energy proposes to truck wastes to a Waste Isolation Pilot Plant (WIPP), located in southeastern New Mexico midway between Carlsbad and Hobbs, and slated to become the world's first nuclear waste repository. Picked in 1975 after attempts to locate a waste site elsewhere failed due to technical and political opposition, construction of WIPP began in 1981.

The waste disposal level is 2,100 feet underground and will consist of 60 rooms, each about 300 feet long, 33 feet wide and 13 feet high, spread across 100 acres. It will dispose of six million cubic feet of materials used in producing nuclear bombs contaminated by plutonium and other radionuclides as well as hazardous chemicals. The waste will be trucked to WIPP over a 35-year period from 10 sites.

This site is unsuitable for long-term storage because it is surrounded by oil and natural gas drill holes, as well as bore holes for potash mining, raising the possibility that brine and other materials injected into these holes could find their way into and through the WIPP storage rooms, releasing radioactive materials into the environment.

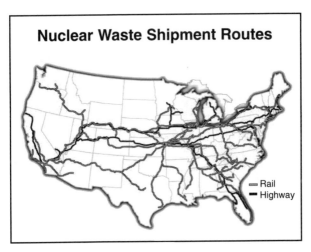

Nuclear Waste Shipment Routes

Rail
Highway

Pete Domenici
Senator from New Mexico

AGE:
64

SALARY
$137,000

EDUCATION:
University of New Mexico

NICKNAME:
St. Pete

CAREER PROFILE:
*Key GOP lawmaker, head
of budget committee and
energy subcommittee*

BEST DEAL WHEELED:
*Saving Los Alamos from
the wrecker's ball and
putting nuclear back on
track*

NOTABLE FACT:
*Sponsored a bill in 1996
that would have
privatized grazing
permits on federal lands*

**BIGGEST
ACCOMPLISHMENT:**
*Making New Mexico
biggest recipient of
federal tax dollars per
capita*

QUOTABLE QUOTE:
"I'm ready to focus on harnessing that [nuclear] genie."

BAD GUY PROFILE:

BUDGET
$16 billion

CEO/SALARY
Bill Richardson
$150,000

HEADQUARTERS
Washington, DC

PRODUCTS
• nuclear weapons
• radioactive waste
• breeder reactors
• R&D for nuclear
  industry

HISTORY
Successor to the Atomic Energy Commission which, along with Admiral Rickover in the Pentagon, created the nuclear power industry. DOE employs over 11,000 federal employees and about 108,000 contract employees, owns and manages over 50 major installations located on 2.4 million acres in 35 states, and is the fourth largest federal landowner in the U.S.

ENVIRONMENTAL RAPSHEET
• After 50 years of nuclear weapons production at scores of sites (one of them, in Idaho, the size of Rhode Island), the government has no credible plan for protecting the environment to assure health and safety of the population. The DOE abandoned its promise to prepare key portions of environmental impact statements that would have put it on the road to a practical program for controlling its wastes. Currently, three quarters of all the nuclear wastes it produces are exempted.
• DOE plans for $40 billion worth of nuclear research over the next decade, including reviving the chemical separation of plutonium. The DOE endorses burning plutonium from dismantled nuclear weapons in commercial nuclear reactors, which will affect the very idea of nuclear non-proliferation, not to mention human health and safety and the environment, creating more nuclear waste at a time the administration has initiated budget cutbacks affecting environmental cleanup programs and wants to open dangerous new waste dumps.

⌐DISHONORABLE MENTION⌐

Nuclear Power

Design & Production
of Nuclear Power
—The Leading U.S. Manufacturers—

General Electric Co.
Headquarters: Fairfield, CT
CEO/Salary: Jack Welch/$8.8 million
Annual Sales: $88 billion
Products: light bulbs, NBC, jet engines, kitchen appliances, nuclear power plants, mutual funds, reinsurance, medical equipment
Lobby spending: $4.8 million
Political Contributions: $660,000

General Atomics
Headquarters: San Diego, CA
CEO/Salary: James N. Blue/salary N/A
Annual Sales: N/A
Products: Energy and defense R&D, primary developers of gas cooled nuclear power technology, largest fusion program in U.S. industry
Lobby spending: $187,000
Political Contributions: $210,000

Major Polluters

HEN THE FEDERAL government took control of the national air and water pollution programs away from the U.S. Public Health Service during the Nixon administration and placed them within a new unit, the Environmental Protection Agency, there was a renewed commitment to regulating environmental pollution.

Sadly that commitment has turned out to be insufficient, scarcely able to keep abreast of expanding industry, and just staying alive in the chilly ideological climate of conservatism with its emphasis on destroying what little exists of regulation. Twenty-five years after the founding of EPA, reports of its do-nothing employees ironically are similar to the complaints against the doctors of the Public Health Service in the 1960s that led to EPA's creation.

Nationally, industry pollutes the air and water with nine billion pounds of toxins a year—about 35 pounds a person. These poisons include PCBs, dioxin, lead, and mercury. They accumulate in the flesh of fish and ultimately of humans and can cause cancer and impair neurological functions.

> Despite the EPA and environmental laws, the vast majority of toxic chemicals have not been fully studied for health and environmental effects.

The truth is that despite the existence of the EPA and the myriad environmental laws and regulations, the vast majority of toxic chemicals have not been fully studied for health and environmen-

Total On- and Off-site Releases
TOP 10 COMPANIES (1996)

COMPANY	POUNDS OF TOXIC RELEASES
Renco Group Inc.	73,000,000
ASARCO Inc.	69,000,000
E.I. DuPont de Nemours & Co.	66,000,000
Potash Corp. of Saskatchewan	54,000,000
Monsanto Co.	40,000,000
General Motors Corp.	37,000,000
International Paper Co.	37,000,000
Cyprus Amax Minerals Co.	30,000,000
Courtaulds United States Inc.	30,000,000
Cytec Industries Inc.	26,000,000
TOTAL OF TOP 10	462,000,000
COUNTRY TOTAL	2,434,000,000

tal effects. According to the Environmental Working Group, a nonprofit research organization that tracks environmental concerns, "TRI (Toxic Release Inventory) records indicate that nearly 30 million pounds of carcinogens, reproductive toxins, or persistent toxic metals were discharged directly to waters. . . . [Eastman Kodak] dumped more cancer causing chemicals into the nation's waters than any other company, 870,000 pounds between 1990 and 1994, according to TRI." All of these discharges went into the Genesee River in New York. The Tennessee Eastman Division of Eastman Chemical, in Kingsport, Tennessee, was the biggest dumper of reproductive toxins—all of them into the Holton River. Bethlehem Steel, Sparrows Point, Maryland dumped more persistently toxic metals than any other polluter, with

Total On- and Off-site Releases
TOP 10 STATES (1996)

STATE	POUNDS OF TOXIC RELEASES
Texas	267,000,000
Louisiana	185,000,000
Ohio	145,000,000
Pennsylvania	122,000,000
Indiana	109,000,000
Illinois	108,000,000
Tennessee	104,000,000
Alabama	103,000,000
Michigan	90,000,000
North Carolina	85,000,000
TOTAL OF TOP 10 STATES	1,318,000,000

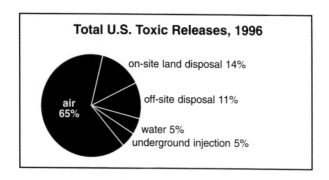

Total U.S. Toxic Releases, 1996

air 65%

on-site land disposal 14%

off-site disposal 11%

water 5%

underground injection 5%

most of them going into the Chesapeake Bay.

Fish, A Key Gauge of Pollution

Fish remain a key gauge of pollution, and people are repeatedly warned to beware of fish from the Great Lakes and their tributaries. In recent years the issuance of fish advisories has become an all too common event. More than 2000 fish advisories are issued every year, a jump of 72 percent since 1993. The main toxins responsible are mercury, PCBs, dioxin, and DDT. Fish from more than 1,700 U.S. waterways are so contaminated with mercury that they should not be eaten or eaten only in limited amounts, according to federal health warnings analyzed by the Environmental Working Group.

> Fish from more than 1,700 U.S. waterways are so contaminated with mercury that they should not be eaten or eaten only in limited amounts.

While continuing industrial pollution exacerbates the damage to fish, much of the poison was dumped into the water years ago and has collected as sediment at the bottom of lakes and streams.

■ Chlorine ■

Chlorine plays a central role in the modern chemical industry as a feedstock for dozens of different products, from
glass to metals. The business is believed to be worth more
than $80 billion in products a year while causing much of the
basic pollution by the chemical industry.

Industrial chlorine is always manufactured in a process
aimed at making something else,
in this case, caustic soda, accom-
plished by running large amounts
of electricity through brine.
(Caustic soda is used in making
bleaches.) Chlorine is created as

> The Cause of Much of the
> Basic Pollution by the
> Chemical Industry

a waste product, and it is only through the ingenuity of modern science that it has found any use at all.

Chlorine is combined with other chemicals, for example
benzene, to make PCBs, which have been used to insulate
different operations in the electrical industry. It makes dioxins which have been used in pesticides. Depending on how it
is used, chlorine can be most toxic to workers, and when released into the atmosphere can result in cancer and attack the
immune system.

Chlorine pollutes the environment during its manufacture (when released into the atmosphere), as waste (when
dumped into the water), and especially when it is destroyed
through incineration where chlorine products always create
dioxins.

CHLORINE PRODUCTS

In the last century, the demand for caustic soda created a
glut of chlorine, exceeding the needs of the existing bleach
markets. The surplus led to a search for new markets, and
chlorine was tried out as a cure-all for all sorts of things: as a
toilet cleaner, moth repellant, disinfectant for coffins. It was
used in medicine as an anaesthetic and soporific, antiseptic
in gynecology and as a mouthwash, as solvent for cleaning
wool, and as paint remover in the metals industry. By the end
of the century factories producing caustic soda were pumping
their chlorine byproduct into the sewer. Herbert Dow, an early
chemical manufacturer, tried to make chlorine into a product
by using it to manufacture bleach for use in textiles and paper.
An unexpected market for chlorine was born in 1915 during
the early days of World War I when the German military unex-

pectedly discovered it was running out of gunpowder. At first the Germans tried to use chemistry to make a synthetic gunpowder, and then turned to producing poisonous chemicals such as chlorine, bromine, and phosgene that could be made into weapons.

While the war briefly alleviated the need for chlorine markets, the public revulsion at chemical warfare cut off that avenue from future expansion. Solvents helped provide a market for a time in making such products as tires, and in dry cleaning. New processes yielded new products, tetraethyl lead, seed disinfectants, wood preservatives, and fungicides, all of them implicated in environmental problems as hazardous waste.

PCBs

Among the most controversial of these products were polychlorinated biphenyls (PCBs), and their history is closely tied to the rise of the automobile. When gasoline was refined from oil, large quantities of benzene were left over, and when benzene was pressurized with chlorine, PCBs resulted. They are a range of compounds—209 in all—that generally take the form of a heavy syrupy liquid. Eric F. Coppolino writes in an excellent explanation of PCBs (*Sierra*, Sept.-Oct. 1994), "They are stable, conduct heat but not electricity, and are not water soluble. As a result they are extremely useful as insulation fluid in electrical transformers and capacitors. They have also been made into plastics and mixed with adhesives, inks, paper, paints, and fabric dyes, with many more tons employed as hydraulic liquids, heat transfer fluids, and lubricating oil in

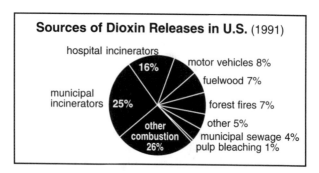

Sources of Dioxin Releases in U.S. (1991)

hospital incinerators 16%
motor vehicles 8%
fuelwood 7%
municipal incinerators 25%
forest fires 7%
other combustion 26%
other 5%
municipal sewage 4%
pulp bleaching 1%

everything from natural gas pipelines to food packing plants. They were once the heating medium of choice in the coils of industrial deep fryers for fish and potato chips, and were even mixed with pesticides and sprayed directly on crops."

> **Not only did the manufacturers know of the dangers, but public health officials were also well aware.**

From the very beginning of the manufacturing process of PCBs, the health of workers was affected because of the toxicity of chlorine. Not only did the manufacturers know of the dangers, but public health officials were also well aware.

It wasn't until the Toxic Substances Act of 1976 that PCBs were finally outlawed. The ban notwithstanding, there are billions of pounds of PCBs still in use in electrical equipment, leaking from landfills and stored up in the fatty tissues of animals where they are passed on through mother's milk and contaminated food to future generations.

DDT, Dioxins, and Agent Orange

Just as scientists and the public were becoming aware of the secret history of PCBs, chlorine was causing a controversy in a different area. For many years pesticides called chlorinated hydrocarbons had been widely used to combat insects on the farm. DDT became the most notorious of these. During their manufacture the process of heating and bonding chlorine with other chemical combinations unintentionally created a group of highly toxic byproducts called dioxins. Dioxin is a common name for a group of chemicals with similar properties and toxicity. There are 75 different kinds of dioxin. The most toxic is 2,3,7,8-tetrachlorodibenzo-p-dioxin or TCDD.

> **A decade after its use in Vietnam, Agent Orange was linked with cancer and birth defects.**

Dioxins are created as byproducts in dozens of chlorine-based industrial chemicals and processes, including pulp and paper bleaching, garbage and hazardous waste incineration, the manufacture of many pesticides and industrial chemicals, certain types of wood preserving, oil refining, and metal smelting.

Dioxin has been building up in the environment since the rapid growth of the chlorinated chemicals industry after World

War II. During the 1960s dioxin-contaminated herbicides were sprayed extensively on forests in the U.S. and other countries. The U.S. military sprayed large amounts of the dioxin-contaminated defoliant Agent Orange in Vietnam. A decade later scientists were beginning to establish links between these chemicals and disease.

In 1979 Dow Chemical scientists linked dioxin exposure to cancer in laboratory animals. Also in that year an EPA study linked miscarriages in Oregon to the spraying of the dioxin-contaminated herbicide 2,4,5-T. EPA suspended use of that herbicide on forest rights of way and pastures. EPA began the process of canceling the pesticide's registration, arguing that no safe level of dioxin exposure can be demonstrated and a total ban was necessary to protect public health. Tests on laboratory animals showed dioxin to be among the most poisonous substances known to science. Doses as low as one trillionth of an animal's body weight have correlated with cancer, birth defects, and reproductive problems. At higher, but still tiny doses it has produced those same effects, plus developmental and nervous and immune system abnormalities, and damage to the kidneys, liver, and skin. A 1985 EPA document regards TCDD as "the most potent carcinogen ever tested in laboratory animals." But even more damaging dioxins not only cause cancers outright, but promote cancers started by other carcinogens, and this is involved in "cancer enhancement." Two decades after Agent Orange was sprayed over Vietnam and over 10 years after the government first discovered and sounded the alert about dioxin's use in pesticides in the U.S., the EPA has yet to devise any regulations to control them.

As for chlorine, despite all efforts, the chemical remains basically unregulated.

Contaminated sediment problems were reported by 23 states.

REFUSE FROM FACTORY FARMS

Now there is a new dimension to the problem in the form of refuse from factory farms that produce hogs and poultry by the millions. Spills from these farms have killed millions of fish from Missouri, Iowa, North Carolina, Virginia, Maryland, and other states.

Recycling also has become a device for the proliferation of toxic pollutants. Under the guise of "recycling," millions of pounds of toxic waste are shipped each year from polluting industries to fertilizer manufacturers and farmers, who used toxic waste laden with dioxin, lead, mercury, and other hazardous chemicals as raw material for fertilizers spread on to U.S. farmland. According to an analysis of federal and state data released by the Environmental Working Group, between 1990 and 1995 more than 450 fertilizer companies or farms in 38 states received numerous shipments of toxic waste.

> Spills from hog and poultry factory farms have killed millions of fish.

Pollution is killing the American fishing industry. Nearly one-third of our shellfish beds are closed or restricted because of bacterial and toxic pollution, and thousands of beaches are closed each year because of contaminated water. This degradation of estuaries will eventually destroy our fisheries since 75 percent of the commercially caught fish are dependent on them. Only Connecticut, Delaware, Illinois, Indiana, New Hampshire, New Jersey, and Ohio comprehensively monitor all their beaches.

> During 1994-1995, 45 million Americans were served drinking water contaminated with fecal matter, parasites, etc.

And land development is drying up millions of acres of wetlands, the swamps that act like sponges, sucking up flood waters and functioning as a natural filtration system for pollutants. Since the 1780s the U.S. has lost over half its wetlands. Under the Clean Water Act, wetland losses have been reduced from half a million acres every year to just over 100,000. But there is little impetus to slow the filling of wetlands. For example, during fiscal 1995 less than 300 individuals—out of the 62,000 who applied—were denied a permit to dredge and fill a wetland.

Drinking water also is endangered. More than 45 million Americans in thousands of communi-

Total Toxic Releases
TOP 10 FACILITIES (1996)

Magnesium Corp. (Rowley, UT)
65 million pounds

ASARCO (E. Helena, MT)
44 million pounds

Zinc Corp. (Monaca, PA)
23 million pounds

Lenzing Fibers (Lowland, TN)
18 million pounds

Courtaulds Fibers (Axis, AL)
28 million pounds

Cyprus Miami Mining (Claypool, AZ)
26 million pounds

Cytec (Westwego, LA)
24 million pounds

Monsanto (Gonzalez, FL)
22 million pounds

DuPont (Victoria, TX)
24 million pounds

PCS Nitrogen Fertilizer (Geismar, LA)
23 million pounds

■ Pollution by Hospitals ■

Lack of basic environmental protective practices at U.S. hospitals is resulting in serious pollution problems and contamination of foods, such as baby foods. The 1998 environmental "Greening" survey of 50 major U.S. hospitals by Health Care Without Harm uncovered widespread failure on the part of medical facilities to take steps to halt contamination of milk, meats, and fish by dioxins and mercury, pollutants that cause a wide range of health impacts.

> Incineration of hospital waste constitutes a major source of dioxin and mercury pollution.

Federal studies have documented that incineration of millions of pounds of hospital waste each year constitutes a major source of both of these pollutants, as well as other environmental contaminants. A Consumer Reports laboratory study in June 1998 found dioxin in processed meat baby food products at levels 100 times higher than the government's current daily limit for this potent carcinogen and hormone disrupting pollutant. A December 1997 government study estimated that 1.6 million women of child-bearing age are potentially exposed each year to unsafe levels of neurotoxic mercury from fish alone, including canned tuna. Thirty-nine state departments of health have issued fish consumption warnings due to mercury contamination.

The "Greening" Hospitals report finds that though the health care industry has already gone a long way to cleaning up its act, they still have a long way to go:

• Just 20 percent of the survey respondents have programs to reduce purchases of polyvinyl chloride (PVC) plastic, which creates dioxin in incinerators. But only 6 percent of the hospitals use PVC-free intravenous bags and all of the hospitals that claim to have PVC reduction programs use PVC intravenous bags.

• Nearly 80 percent of the survey respondents say that they have mercury reduction programs, but 37 percent of these hospitals still buy patient thermometers that contain mercury and nearly half buy mercury blood pressure devices.

• While most (80 percent) hospitals conducted waste surveys and trained their staff in how to handle infectious waste, over 40 percent of survey respondents continue to incinerate medical waste that should be treated by safer methods.

• The average hospital is only recycling about one-third of the readily recyclable items.

ties were served drinking water during 1994–1995 that was polluted with fecal matter, parasites, disease-causing microbes, radiation, pesticides, toxic chemicals, and lead at levels that violated health standards established under the federal Safe Drinking Water Act. More than 18,000 public water supplies reported at least one violation of a federal drinking water health standard during this two-year period.

INDUSTRY AND GOVERNMENT IGNORE THE LAWS

Laws on the books are ignored. Nearly 20 percent of the nation's 6900 major industrial, municipal, and federal facilities were in significant noncompliance with the Clean Water Act during at least one quarter from January 1995 through March 1996. Additionally 32 percent of all major industrial dischargers violated their permit during the first quarter of 1996, with 21 percent committing serious, potentially environmentally harmful pollution violations.

The EPA's enforcement record has slipped. Between 1994 and 1996 EPA lawsuits against polluters have dropped by 44 percent and EPA's Clean Water Act permit inspections are down by 31 percent. In a series of reports in 1998 the Inspector General of the EPA found that state and federal officials routinely failed to enforce the pollution laws. Sewage treatment plants operated with obsolete permits or none at all, while inspectors simply never checked if factories met standards. The states, which actu-

> Nearly 20 percent of the nation's 6900 major industrial, municipal, and federal facilities were in significant noncompliance with the Clean Water Act.

■■■ The Racial Bias of Pollution ■■■

Each year the U.S. generates 2.8 billion pounds of toxic waste. A 1987 report by the United Church of Christ found that hazardous waste-generating plants are twice as likely to be located in communities with high populations of blacks and Hispanics.

Nowhere is this trend more starkly illustrated than in St. James Parish, Louisiana, in the heart of "cancer alley." It already harbors 11 chemical plants that emit 24 million pounds of toxins a year, including Occidental, Freeport McMoRan, Chevron, and Texaco. The parish is also home to the IMC-Agrico Fertilizer plant, which, until its operations were curtailed in 1995, held the distinction of being the most toxic plant in America, discharging 174 million pounds of poisons into the Mississippi every year. For more than a decade, St. James Parish ranked as the most polluted county in America.

> For more than a decade, St. James Parish ranked as the most polluted county in America.

St. James is one of the poorest parishes in Louisiana and the small towns near the cluster of chemical plants are nearly all black. Less than 50 percent of the children in the area graduate from high school. More than 60 percent of the residents are unemployed. The average per capita income is $7,200. The cancer rate in St. James is among the highest in Louisiana, a state that ranks fifth in the nation in cancer deaths.

These statistics made St. James attractive to the Shintech Corporation, a Japanese chemical company looking for a place to build one of the world's largest polyvinyl chloride plants. In 1996 Louisiana Governor Mike Foster offered Shintech an amazing trove of inducements to build its plant in St. James. Most alluring was the $120 million in property tax relief and enterprise zone tax credits—that's nearly $800,000 for each full-time job produced by the plant.

Just when the Shintech plant seemed a sure thing, enter the Tulane University Environmental Law Clinic, a largely student-run operation which filed an environmental justice complaint with the Environmental Protection Agency on behalf of St. James residents. The first-of-a-kind petition charged that EPA should deny Shintech a federal air pollution permit because toxic emissions from the factory would disproportionately harm the poor and people of color. This act of defiance enraged Gov. Foster, who attacked the law clinic. Foster fumed that he would revoke Tulane University's tax status, demanded that clinic lawyers be investigated for "barratry" (vexatious incitement to litigation) and urged the New Orleans Business Roundtable to suspend contributions to the university until the Law Clinic was brought to its knees.

> The EPA ruled that the eight million pounds of poisonous chemicals that will fall yearly on the black residents of St. James Parish will not violate their constitutional rights.

The university held firm, but the Clinton Administration caved in. Under pressure from Louisiana senator John Breaux, a conservative Democrat, the EPA ruled that the eight million pounds of poisonous chemicals a year that will fall on the black residents of St. James Parish from the Shintech plant will not violate their constitutional rights. It's now up to the federal courts to determine whether it's legal for polluting companies to site their plants based on the racial composition of communities.

In September of 1998 the company indicated it would try to avoid further legal confrontation and build the plant near Baton Rouge.

ally administer the programs, fell short of federal goals. For example, according to a June 1998 *New York Times* report, "In Idaho and Alaska, the EPA's regional office in Seattle had written 33 permits in two and a half years, but there was a backlog of 1,000 permit applications."

In air pollution, the Clinton administration has been struggling to clean up an especially deadly form of air pollution, the tiny particles that penetrate deep into human lungs, claiming the lives of more than 64,000 Americans every year. The administration argues that if these rules are adopted they will halve the premature deaths from particulate air pollution, saving 20,000 people. They can reduce the incidence of acute childhood respiratory problems by more than a quarter of a million occurrences every year, and cut chronic bronchitis by 60,000 cases every year, and in general cut down emergency room visits and childhood illnesses. In addition, they can cut haze and visibility problems by as much as 77 percent in some areas such as national parks.

Residents of communities of color in California will be among the prime beneficiaries of the proposal. An Environmental Working Group analysis of air pollution data from 161 locations across the state shows that residents of communities of color are nearly three times more likely to breathe

> Residents of communities of color are nearly three times more likely to breathe dangerous levels of air pollution than Californians living in predominantly white communities.

dangerous levels of air pollution than Californians living in predominantly white communities. According to the 1990 census, 42 percent of the population of California was classified as Hispanic, black, Asian, native American, or another non white race. ☠

Ira Rennert
CEO, Renco Group, New York, NY

AGE:
63

EDUCATION:
Brooklyn College

NICKNAME:
Lord Rennert

BUSINESS PROFILE:
Controls 95 percent of Renco Group, private holding company, which through subsidiaries makes the HumVee, controls lead mines in Missouri and Peru and owns Magnesium Corp of America, the largest single source of air pollution in America and the source of 95 percent of all the air pollution in the state of Utah where its plant is based.

THE VINDICATOR

BEST DEAL WHEELED:
Being at top of EPA's toxic polluter list and getting away with it.

MOST IMAGINATIVE SIDELINE:
Building biggest contemporary residence in America on Long Island for more than $100 million.

NOTABLE FACT:
Major supporter of Israel premier Benjamin Netanyahu and helped fund the long blocked tunnel near Jerusalem's Wailing Wall, setting off worst riots since start of peace process.

QUOTABLE QUOTE:
Rennert does not give interviews, but Mag Corp spokesman Lee Brown said, "I am sick and tired of being picked on" by "unqualified, mean-spirited, ignorant individuals" attacking the company.

BAD GUY PROFILE:

ANNUAL SALES
$1.2 billion (1995)

Potash Corporation
of Saskatchewan Inc.

HEADQUARTERS
Saskatoon,
Canada

CEO/SALARY
Charles E. Childers
salary: N/A

PRODUCTS
• nitrogen fertilizer
• nitrogen chemicals
• phosphate products

**POLITICAL
CONTRIBUTIONS**
• N/A

ENVIRONMENTAL RAPSHEET
• In 1994 Louisiana ordered Potash's U.S. affiliate, Arcadian, to equip its Geismar plant with pollution control equipment, and it added systems to control groundwater contamination in Memphis.
• Iowa launched a 1990 investigation because of nitrates in groundwater at Clinton.
• Ohio has moved to tighten control over groundwater discharges at the Lima plant.
• The Port Authority of New York sued the company for damages, alleging that Arcadian—as a manufacturer of ammonium nitrate—was liable for damages in the World Trade towers blast.
• In 1993 the Justice Department initiated a grand jury investigation into ammonium-nitrate pricing practices in the explosives industry.
• OSHA proposes to fine the company $4 million for an incident at its Lake Charles plant.

OTHER POINTS OF INTEREST
• One of the world's largest integrated fertilizer and feed product companies, it accounts for 16 percent of the global potash business, produces 9 percent of the world's phosphates, and is the largest nitrogen producer in the western hemisphere.
• Through Arcadian, Potash Corporation has a deep water port at its Geismar plant in Louisiana. It owns or leases 50 terminal facilities, and operates about 1300 railcars. A plant in Trinidad supplies customers in Latin America, Europe, and Africa as well as the U.S.

MONSANTO

Food · Health · Hope™

ANNUAL SALES
$7.5 billion

CEO/SALARY
Robert B. Shapiro
$2.7 million

PRODUCTS
• herbicides
• insecticides
• fertilizers
• pharmaceuticals
• NutraSweet
• soap

HEADQUARTERS
St. Louis, MO

POLITICAL CONTRIBUTIONS
• $130,000

LOBBY FEES
• $2.5 million

ENVIRONMENTAL RAPSHEET
• Searle, a Monsanto subsidiary, faces personal injury suits in U.S. and abroad in connection with manufacture of IUD, which it no longer sells, as well as class action suits alleging antitrust violations for providing rebates to HMOs and other large purchasers.
• Monsanto faces suits over patents for cotton and corn that contain a gene encoding for Bacillus thuringiensis (Bt) endotoxin.
• The Georgia Environmental Protection Division charged the company with violations at its NutraSweet plant, and Monsanto agreed to pay $99,000 and install environmental improvements costing $120,000.

OTHER POINTS OF INTEREST
• Founded in 1901 to manufacture saccharin, Monsanto began producing plastics in the 1930s.
• In the 1970s it concentrated on specialty chemicals, engineered products (silicon wafers), and biologically-based products (herbicides and insecticides).
• Monsanto has been the largest producer for the soap and detergent industry in the U.S.
• It manufactures pharmaceuticals such as aspirin and acetaminophen.
• Monsanto, a leader in agricultural biotechnology, set about to experiment with genetically engineering new disease resistant plants.

BAD GUY PROFILE:

ANNUAL SALES
$45 billion

HEADQUARTERS
Wilmington, DE

PRODUCTS
- Conoco
- Lycra, Dacron
- Teflon, Codura
- herbicides
- Mylar
- pharmaceuticals

CEO/SALARY
Charles Holliday
$1.1 million

POLITICAL CONTRIBUTIONS
- $150,000

LOBBY FEES
- $960,000

ENVIRONMENTAL RAPSHEET
- DuPont is the number two water polluter and number three air polluter in the country.
- Involved in 700 suits from growers who claimed its Benlate 50 DF fungicide had caused crop damage.
- Defendant in lawsuits alleging property damage resulting from leaks in polybutylene plumbing systems.
- Conoco accused in Colorado of violating RCRA, and in California of violating hazardous waste regulations.
- In 1994 the EPA filed a complaint against DuPont proposing to assess $1.9 million in penalties for distributing triazine herbicide with wrong product labels.
- In 1995 the EPA charged the company failed to provide notice of chlorine emissions from an Ohio plant; an illegal oleum release charged in Kentucky.
- In 1996 the Justice Department notified Conoco of its intention to file suit under the Clean Water Act for damages caused by illegal releases from 1991 to 1994.
- Charged by West Virginia in 1996 for landfill violations.
- In 1994 residents near the Pompton Lakes, NJ, explosives plant charged DuPont with negligence, fraud, wrongful death. This follows a $38 million settlement over ground water contamination with high levels of mercury and lead.

OTHER POINTS OF INTEREST
- With about 300 descendants of Irénée du Pont de Nemours still owning a total of 15 percent of the world's largest chemical company.

CYTEC

ANNUAL SALES
$1.2 billion

HEADQUARTERS
West Paterson, NJ

CEO/SALARY
Darryl D. Fry
$1.7 million

PRODUCTS
• aerospace
  materials
• paper chemicals
• mining chemicals
• resin products

POLITICAL CONTRIBUTIONS
• N/A

LOBBY FEES
• N/A

ENVIRONMENTAL RAPSHEET

• Defendant in 12 cases in Texas in which plaintiffs seek damages for injuries allegedly due to exposure to benzene, butadiene, asbestos, or other chemicals.
• In Pennsylvania 26 employees of Boeing-Vertol allege exposure to asbestos-containing products.
• Defendant in a class action in Jefferson Parish, LA, where residents claim damages caused by a sulfur dioxide emission in 1992 from the Fortier facility.
• Defendant in two class actions by people alleging injury as the result of an explosion and fire at the firm's Fortier plant.
• Defendant in five suits in New York and Ohio regarding lead-based paints.
• The EPA is demanding $420,000 in penalties for improper use of the firm's industrial furnace at its Kalamazoo, MI, plant.
• In Louisiana, environmentalists are fighting the company's use of deep well disposal at Fortier.

OTHER POINTS OF INTEREST

• About 60 percent of the company's business comes from chemicals used in treating waste water and sludge, and for the manufacture of paper and separating minerals from raw ore in mining. Its chemicals are used in cosmetics, making paints and inks, and chemicals used in semiconductor manufacture. A quarter of its business comes from aerospace work, chemicals employed as adhesives and in making composites.

P A R T 3

Behind-the-Scenes Players

Lobbyists

HERE ARE PROBABLY UPWARDS of 10,000 Washington lobbyists, people who influence government on behalf of a client's interests. They make anywhere from $100,000 to $1 million a year and congregate around the downtown K Street corridor, chockablock with law offices, PR companies, pollsters, media consultants, and outposts of foundations. Ninety firms earned at least $1 million in lobby fees in 1997, according to *Legal Times*.

According to the Center for Responsive Politics, the good government group and a major source of information on money and politics, lobbyists spent $1.2 billion trying to set policy last year. Their main target is the $170 billion in "fiscal incentives," "export promotion support," and other major subsidies—corporate welfare. That figure dwarfs the $75 billion allocated during the same period for social welfare programs.

The old fashioned method of paying off politicians—trips and women—has been replaced by "fact-finding missions," where representatives make speeches at cushy resorts, and phony "astroturf lobbying," where banks of telemarketing operators persuade citizens to send letters or wire members of Congress on one issue or another.

> The old fashioned method of paying off politicians—trips and women—has been replaced by "fact-finding missions."

According to the *Wall Street Journal*, 40 percent of Congressional incumbents who were defeated in 1992 went on to become lobbyists. Between 1988 and 1993, 42 percent of all Senate committee staff directors later became lobbyists, while the corre-

Political Action Committee Contributions

Top 5 **Chemical** PACs: $1,000,000
(DuPont, Monsanto, ICI, Eastman, Dow)

Top 5 **Timber** PACs: $1,600,000
(International Paper, Weyerhaeuser, Champion, Georgia-Pacific, Stone)

Top 5 **Oil** PACs: $2,100,000
(Exxon, Chevron, Arco, Mobil, Amoco)

Top 5 **Mining** PACs: $500,000
(Asarco, Freeport McMoRan, Phelps-Dodge, FMC)

Top 5 **Solid Waste** PACs: $1,000,000
(BFI, WMX, Ogden, USA Waste, Allwaste)

Top 5 **Agribusiness** PACs: $970,000
(Cargill, ADM, ConAgra, IBP, Tyson)

Top 5 **Energy** PACs: $1,400,000
(Enron, PG&E, Edison Intl., Duke Power, Entergy)

*All **Environmental** Group PACs:* $2,300,000

Monsanto Corporation, E.I. Dupont de Nemours and Co, Dow Agro-Sciences, and 32 other manufacturers of pesticides for home and garden use have banded together for lobbying purposes in an organization that calls itself Responsible Industry for a Sound Environment. All told, RISE and its member firms spent more than $15 million in 1996 to employ 219 Washington lobbyists, including 24 former House staff members, 22 former Senate staff members, 10 former executive branch officials, nine former White house aides, four former Representatives, and three former Senators.

—Center for Public Integrity, 1998

sponding number on the House side was 34 percent. Meanwhile, between 1974 and 1990 half of the senior officials who left the U.S. Trade Representatives office went to work as shills for foreign companies and governments.

GREENWASHING

Greenwashing—the use of public relations to transform a polluting company into a seemingly ecologically friendly one—has become a vast environmental lobby seeking to advance a new green-friendly face of industry.

> Transforming A Polluting Company into a Seemingly Eco-Friendly One

Greenwashing is so successful that nearly all companies claim to be dedicated to the environment and 90 percent of Americans claim to be environmentalists. To hear people talk, you'd never know there was anything wrong. Indeed, with each passing Earth Day, a fresh spate of articles and books appears celebrating the U.S.'s great success in overcoming the environmental dilemmas of our times.

Schools Lobby for Timber

In 1908 the timber industry pushed a bill through Congress requiring the Forest Service to turn over 25 percent of all gross receipts from timber sales on the national forest to local counties. The money was to used to fund county road projects and school programs. This program had the effect of making many school systems in the West dependent on timber sale receipts. In fact, through the 1980s and early 1990s when Forest Service timber sales were at their peak, this fund was generating nearly half a billion dollars a year for public schools. Thus, school superintendents became one of the timber industry's most ardent lobbyists. In 1991, school districts in Oregon and Washington submitted testimony to Congress opposing the listing of the spotted owl as a threatened species on the grounds that cut-backs in logging rates to save the owl would decimate their school budgets.

In return, many schools in rural districts have invited the timber industry into the classroom. One timber industry sponsored program is called Project Learning Tree. Funded by Weyerhaeuser, Louisiana-Pacific, and International Paper, Project Learning Tree provides lesson plans for courses in biology, ecology, and natural history from kindergarten through middle school. One Project Learning Tree program teaches children that forests need to be frequently logged to keep them in healthy condition.

Jack O'Dwyer, the chronicler of the public relations business, listed 42 public relations companies that have made a special business of greenwashing. *PR Watch*, an industry watchdog, reports that in 1990 alone, U.S. businesses spent about $500 million to hire the services of anti-environmental PR professionals. Greenwashing has become just another part of business, and one that consumers pay for.

To become a serious player in the greenwash business, you start out by currying favor with the big environmental groups through contributions and gimmicky joint ventures to show just how much you care—things like saving dolphins, planting new trees, and recycling plastics. Then you fashion your own message. According to DC-based PR consultant E. Bruce Harrison, the PR counselors should go "beyond scrambling" into "risk communication." In any environmental crisis, Harrison advises his corporate clients to follow "the basics of crisis communication" the pros learned from the Exxon Valdez disaster: "Get to the scene. Respond to media questions immediately . . . demonstrate that the company cares."

> Polluting companies curry favor with big environmental groups through contributions.

Mining and Academe

Under the 1872 Mining Law, the U.S. government is not allowed to charge royalties on minerals removed from federal lands, but most western states impose fees for mining on state-owned lands. In Montana, a hefty share of the royalties go back to the mining school at Montana Tech University in Butte. The haul can be quite lucrative. The royalties to Montana Tech from a single mine, the 7-Up/Pete Mine near Helena, is estimated at more than $60 million. The president of Montana Tech is Dr. Lindsay Norman. In 1988, Norman was invited to join the board of directors of Pegasus Gold, a Canadian-owned firm that operates the huge Zortman-Landusky gold mine in northern Montana. For his services as a director, Norman was paid more than $40,000 a year in directors' fees. In 1996, Montana environmentalists put forth on the ballot an initiative that would have imposed stringent new standards on mining for the state. Norman rushed forth to offer his professional opinion as a scientist that the new regulations were unnecessary. After leading in early polls by a wide margin, the measure, thanks to an aggressive public relations campaign suggesting that the initiative was "regulatory overkill," went down to defeat.

As *PR Watch* reported, PR firms are busy helping industry set up community advisory panels "to
strengthen their image in towns and neighborhoods
that host industrial facilities." Soon, average citizens will be able to plug in through a phonebook to
a conference call with the caring company executive. The "suit" will sympathize, but remind them
about the jobs they may lose by pushing the com-

Lobbyists Without Principle

On occasion, members of Congress—to promote their own
interests—hire lobbyists. Former Louisiana Senator
Bennett Johnston ceaselessly promoted the interests of the
energy industry, but when his pro-industry bill got bogged down
in a 1991 debate, he hired a former Carter aide Anne Wexler.
So when Johnston invited 150 utility executives, lobbyists for
manufacturing companies, and energy associations to a meeting to seek support for his bill, he was flanked by W. Henson
Moore, the deputy energy secretary in Bush's cabinet, and
Wexler.

This was a switch for Wexler, who only a few days before
had been lobbying on behalf of a group of utilities against the
legislation because it was "anti-consumer" and spelled "chaos"
for the utility business. Then, Wexler made an "executive deci-
sion" to accept the assignment from Johnston "because it was
the right thing to do."

Among other things, the bill would have opened the Arctic
National Wildlife Refuge to oil drilling, sped up the licensing of
nuclear power plants, partially deregulated electric utilities, and
encouraged the building of natural gas pipelines. As for Wexler's
views on these matters, her colleague Tom Gibson, speaking in
lobbyese, told the *Washington Post*, "there was a general recognition that the environmental groups had been effective in twisting the focus [of the debate]. . . . It was felt that more had to be
done to return the issues to broad national focus. At some point
in that recognition, it was felt that the Wexler group was uniquely
equipped to bring together a broad coalition." Wexler's assignment, Johnston said, was "America needs a broad energy bill.
You work it out."

---

pany too far.

The idea is to change public perception both about the environment and the polluters. Hence journalists are key targets to help companies deliver their message. Today there are a variety of PR firms that offer background information on environmental journalists—sort of a cross between a credit check and the House Un-American Activities file. As one service advertised: "Not only will you find news on journalists, we'll tell you what they want from you and what strategies you can employ with them to generate more positive stories and better manage potentially negative situations."

There are other, more subtle, ways of changing

AP/WIDE WORLD PHOTOS

Lobbyist and Al Gore fundraiser Peter Knight.

the way journalists look at companies engaged in the environment. According to *Environment Writer*, DuPont flacks invited selected members of the media to help the company figure out a PR strategy for its pesticides. As the flacks set out the program, "this learning endeavor will be used to help DuPont es-

---

The Illusion of Grassroots Support

When corporations don't buy votes outright, they go to elaborate lengths to create the illusion that the grassroots democratic process backs their policies. In 1991 auto interests hired Bonner & Associates, a Washington firm that "specializes in organizing and conducting grassroots campaigns at the federal and state levels." The company's clients include Philip Morris, Exxon, and Chase Manhattan Bank. In March of 1990, *Common Cause* reported, the firm got together the leaders of several local groups for a press conference in the Dirksen Senate Office building. The meeting was organized by E. Bruce Harrison, the environmental PR man who got his start in the 1960s as a flack for the chemical industry against Rachel Carson, and Senators Donald Riegel of Michigan and Don Nickles of Oklahoma. Bonner had contacted farm, religious, minority business, youth, and other groups to warn them the proposed fuel efficiency measures would be a disaster for them.

"Jack Bonner, president of Bonner & Associates, says his firm was 'very up-front' about working for the auto industry. Bonner flew in the heads of the Florida Silver-haired Legislature (a seniors' group), the Nebraska Farm Bureau, a Big Brothers/Big Sisters chapter and an official of the National Sheriff's Association. Bonner also persuaded Linda Werkmeister, then head of client services at South Dakota's Easter Seals, to explain how the proposed legislation would harm her organization's efforts to help disabled people," *Common Cause* reported.

The only problem was that Easter Seals had no position on the Bryan bill. Warned not to participate, Werkmeister was fired after she appeared at the press conference. Getting dragged into the debate was an embarrassment for Easter Seals, according to the director of its national office, because the group tries to stay clear of political causes not directly involved in its work. Joe Romer, the director, told *Common Cause* he resented the fact that "corporate interests try to manipulate and use small nonprofits like ours . . . as a pawn in a political battle not related to people with disabilities."

---

tablish new policies regarding pesticides: their use and information important to consumers, the government, farmers and the press . . . Your ethics as journalists (and that of your news organization) will not be violated or jeopardized in any way . . . The goal is to make better pesticide policies."

According to one participant, "they would give us small pieces of paper which would say something like, 'DuPont makes very wonderful chemicals, and no one needs to worry.'" The journalists were asked to concoct a storyline from information on the sheet of paper, while the DuPont researchers intently watched them from behind one-way mirrors. When their work was finished, the reporters were given envelopes containing $250 in cash.

> The company and government spokespeople did what they had learned: convey as little information as possible in as many words as possible.

In another incident, Dashka Slater described in *Sierra* magazine how she was hired by a Houston-based consulting firm to play the part of the "predatory press," in a staged oil spill. Professional actors played environmentalists while Arco employees and government officials played themselves. "The drills give company flacks the opportunity to practice varnishing the truth just in case the mop-up doesn't go as planned," Slater wrote. "Mostly the company and government spokespeople did what they had learned to do in numerous media-training workshops: convey as little information as possible in as many words as possible." ☠

■ Lobbyists Writing Legislation ■

No sooner had the Republican-controlled Congress started in 1995 than the corporations began writing and organizing the passage of legislation. For example, lobbyists for electric utilities drafted legislation to roll back regulations and rounded up members to get it passed. Here's what happened:

To oversee the legislation, Senate Majority Leader Bob Dole hired Kyle McSlarrow, a lawyer from Hunton & Williams, a Richmond-based firm that was lobbying the measure. McSlarrow had run twice for Congress and lost, then joined Dole's staff. Before doing so, however, he paid off his debt by raising thousands of dollars in campaign contributions from companies with a special interest in regulatory relief.

As the bill came before his Judiciary Committee, Chairman Orrin Hatch took charge of revisions, but was sharply criticized for overly relying on lobbyists. Among them were Roger Marzulla, a Bush-era Justice Department official, representing Hoechst-Celanese, a chemical firm that stood to gain in several court cases if the bill passed. Another was Barbara Bankoff, a former Carter-era EPA official, representing Eli Lilly and Siemens. In addition, C. Boyden Gray, Bush's counsel in the White House and now an attorney with Wilmer, Cutler & Pickering, wrote the original bill. Gray's presence was vital because under Reagan he had written seminal legislation mandating cost-benefit ratios by bureaucrats drawing up federal regulations. He sought to extend cost-benefit analysis to regs in air pollution that corporations anticipated would cost them dearly.

Enter Kyle McSlarrow. He said he had not been lobbied by members of his former firm since he left its employ. But his former boss, George Freeman—a partner in the firm with decades of experience lobbying on behalf of electric utilities—was among those invited by Hatch's staff to brief Judiciary Committee aides on the Dole bill on March 29, 1996.

David S. Cloud of the *Congressional Quarterly* writes, "In an interview, Freeman said he made clear at the briefing that he was not there representing clients, but in his capacity as chairman of the American Bar Association's regulatory reform task force, a group working to improve the Dole bill. Two other Hunton & Williams partners were there representing clients and made that known. One of them had previously solicited clients, promising, according to the *New York Times,* "quiet, behind-the-scenes intervention" on regulatory legislation.

■ Trade Associations ■

American Mining Congress
1920 N St. NW, Washington, DC 20036
DIRECTOR: John Knebel
BUDGET: $7 million
STAFF: 50
PROFILE: The AMC, founded in 1897, now represents more than 400 mining companies, many of them based in Canada; maintains a large political action committee and has been a key funder of the Wise Use Movement in the western U.S.
ISSUES: Fighting off reform of the General Mining Law of 1872; also lobbies against strengthening clean water laws and the endangered species act.

American Petroleum Institute
2215 Constitution Ave., NW, Washington, DC 20005
DIRECTOR: Charles DiBona
BUDGET: $85 million
Staff: 455
PROFILE: Since 1919, API has been one of the most aggressive and effective trade associations in Washington; acts as a lobbying and public relations firm for all the major oil companies, independent producers and service station owners; doles out more than $87,000 a year in soft money contributions to Democratic and Republican parties.
ISSUES: Fought off fuel efficiency standards; preserved multibillion dollar depletion allowance tax break for oil companies; ran national campaign against new smog rules by EPA; subverted global warming treaty; lobbied for increased oil and gas drilling on public lands.

American Forest and Paper Association
1111 19th St., NW, Washington, DC
President: Henson Moore
BUDGET: $50 million
STAFF: 190
PROFILE: The timber industry's lobbying and PR outfit; represents more than 1,500 forest products and paper companies; employs more than 40 lobbyists on its staff and retains the services of 11 more outside lobby shops, including Steven Quarles and Clinton friend Anne Wexler; its PAC doled out more than $200,000 in the 1996 elections.
ISSUES: Lobbies on a full gamut of environmental issues, from

endangered species, such as the spotted owl and grizzly, to clean water and air pollution laws that affect pulp mills and other timber plants; also pro-active, pushing legislation to exempt so-called salvage logging on national forest lands from all environmental laws; the most aggressive opponent of new national park and wilderness area proposals.

Chemical Manufacturers Association

1300 Wilson Blvd., Arlington, VA 22209
DIRECTOR: Frederick Webber
BUDGET: $28 million
STAFF: 285
PROFILE: Represents the interests of more than 250 chemical companies, including Canadian firms. One legislative aide said, "Only the tobacco lobby throws their weight around as hard as the CMA."
ISSUES: Ardent foe of environmental regulations relating to clean air, clean water and hazardous waste laws; supports replacing regulatory approach with cost/benefit analysis and risk assessment. Uses its "independent research" to aggressively attack environmentalists and government scientists who link chemical exposure to cancer.

Edison Electric Institute

701 Pennsylvania Ave., NW, Washington, DC 20004
DIRECTOR: Thomas Kuhn
BUDGET: $70 million
STAFF: 300
PROFILE: Formed in 1970; the major trade association and lobbying arm for the nation's electric utilities representing more than 160 companies; controls the Power Political Action Committee; has recently retained the services of former Minnesota congressman, Vin Webber, as its key lobbyist on Capitol Hill.
ISSUES: One of the hottest topics in Washington during the late 1990s has been deregulation of electric utilities; lobbied fiercely for deregulation bills that would allow utilities to soak ratepayers with so-called "stranded costs," the billions utilities have spent on ailing nuclear plants and outdated and polluting coal-fired generators.

National Association of Homebuilders

1201 15th St. NW, Washington, DC 20005
DIRECTOR: Kent Colton

BUDGET: $35 million

STAFF: 255

PROFILE: The main lobbying shop for the building trades. It represents 155,000 builders and building companies. It operates the powerful BUILD-PAC and doles out hundreds of thousands a year in soft money.

ISSUES: Successfully lobbied for a moratorium on new listings under Endangered Species Act in 1995; staunch opponent of wetlands protection; opposes preservation of old-growth forest; underwrites takings lawsuits.

National Cattleman's Association

PO Box 3469, Englewood, CO 80155

Executive Vice-President: Burton Eller

BUDGET: $12 million

STAFF: 70

PROFILE: Represents ranchers, beef producers, cattle breeders and feeders. Cattlemen's Association is a key backer of Wise Use movement.

ISSUES: Battles yearly to keep grazing fees on public lands far below market rates; supports roll-back of Endangered Species Act; opposes application of Clean Water Act standards to cattle operations; backed legal attack on "Oprah" for her show on mad cow disease; supported ouster of reform-minded Jim Baca as head of Bureau of Land Management.

Nuclear Energy Institute

1776 Eye Street, NW, Washington, DC 20006

DIRECTOR: Joe Colvin

BUDGET: $20 million

STAFF: 150

PROFILE: Represents nuclear power utilities, the three big nuclear reactor builders (Westinghouse, General Electric and ABB-Combustion Engineering), power plant construction firms, such as Bechtel, labor unions and quasi-government entities with a stake in nuclear power, such as the Tennessee Valley Authority.

ISSUES: Lobbied aggressively for the Yucca Mountain nuclear waste storage site in Nevada; used the global warming issue to campaign for increased federal money for nuclear power; backed sale of American nuclear plants to China and Ukraine; ran a futile campaign against the TV show *The Simpsons* for its negative portrayal of nuclear power

Lobbyist Ћall of Ƒame

MARK REY helped write the legendary salvage logging bill. Touted in the press as a way to reduce the risk of forest fires in the West, it contained small print that had nothing to do with fires, but required the Forest Service to sell healthy stands of trees, including some of the oldest groves in America. Moreover, the measure

> The Most Adroit Forest Industry Lobbyist in Washington

exempted all these sales from compliance with federal environmental laws. The bill was signed into law by President Clinton in 1995, who later claimed that he had been deceived.

Rey then crafted a series of legislative initiatives to expand logging on the vast Tongass National Forest of Alaska. One of those measures was designed to extend by 15 years the contract for Tongass timber held by the Ketchikan Pulp, a subsidiary of Louisiana Pacific. Senator Murkowski (R-AK) had a personal stake in the passage of this legislation. At the time these measures were being drafted and debated, Murkowski owned stock in both Louisiana Pacific and Ketchikan State Bank, the pulp mill's debt holder. In 1997 Rey described how the Republican leadership proposed to rewrite basic laws governing the nation's forests. The timber companies want to get rid of the minimum requirements for species in the forests, and eliminate prohibitions on below-cost timber sales.

Though the salvage rider expired at the end of 1996, a few days later Sen. Larry Craig (D-ID), chairman of the Subcommittee on Forests, was back with a new piece of legislation to make many of the most anti-environmental provisions of the salvage rider permanent. The bill offered by Senator Craig closely mirrors recommendations presented to the Senate Agriculture Committee by Steven Quarrles, a lobbyist for the American Forest and Paper Association, the $50-million-a-year trade association for the timber industry. Craig's bill would require the Forest Service and Bureau of Land Management to make resource extraction activities, such as logging, mining, and grazing, the dominant use of America's federal forests, jettisoning the century-old philosophy of multiple-use, which held that public lands should be for a variety of values including wildlife, recreation, and scenic beauty. The bill would also prohibit legal challenges of timber sales and mining activities for violations of the Clean Water Act and other environmental laws.

BIRCH BAYH rescued the giant Canadian Noranda mining company from a big gold mining deal near Yellowstone National park that was bogged down by attacks from environmentalists who charged that the mine would end up polluting the nation's first and grandest national park.

> Former Democratic Senator from Indiana, Now Mining and Manufacturing Lobbyist

Noranda's subsidiary Battle Mountain Gold had put together an enticing deal by assembling a series of leases on public lands under the 1872 Mining Act which allows the staking of mining leases for $5 an acre, with no royalties. But Noranda had a miserable environmental record, and environmentalists fought the company's Yellowstone project on grounds it would end up polluting the nation's first and grandest national park.

Earlier in 1997 Noranda employed Bayh for $120,000, along with former Montana governor Tim Babcock, to extract the best deal possible for them in Washington.

Though the 1872 Mining Act offers ample opportunities for making a good profit, Clinton offered Noranda a much better deal: $65 million in other federal properties and a grant of immunity from prosecution for civil and criminal penalties amounting to $135 million for their previous activities on the mining site, where many of the streams were rendered highly acidic. As an added bonus the mining company will be able to take a $30 million tax write-off, another subsidy paid for by American taxpayers. In total the package amounts to a $230 million pay off to a renegade mining company that had threatened America's oldest national park with ecological ruin. The President praised the deal as a solution "where everybody wins," saying that it is symbolic of how the environment and the economy can work in harmony.

Bayh interceded in 1997 on behalf of Monon Corp., a semi-tractor trailer manufacturer, in an attempt to reduce a $600,000 fine leveled by the Indiana Environmental Affairs Dept. for mishandling hazardous waste. Bayh justified his actions by saying, "If you can use government influence to achieve a good social purpose, that's exciting." He added, "At the beginning of the meeting I wanted everyone to know that even though my name was the same as the man in the governor's office [his son, Gov. Evan Bayh], they should give that no credence. I'm a lawyer trying to make a living."

DONALD PEARLMAN, who served as assistant secretary of both Energy and Interior departments in the Reagan administration, is by far the energy industry's most effective lobbyist in fighting climate-control rules.

Pearlman works the international conferences through the Kuwaiti and Saudi delegations. He can be seen standing outside the room, a cigarette

> Energy Industry's Most Effective Lobbyist in Fighting Climate-Control Rules

dangling from his lips, greeting the Arabs as they come and go, with a pat on the back or a stern order. Secretive to the extreme, Pearlman seldom talks to the press. He infuriates the environmentalists who call him "Fingers" because of his hair-splitting changes on every document and because he uses tiny discrepancies in documents to drive the climate-change scientists and environmentalists mad.

No less infuriated are members of the U.S. delegation, whose every public utterance finds its way—thanks to Pearlman—onto the desks of the Congressional right-wing the next day. "No battles are won standing on the sidelines," Fingers once admonished the Canadian coal producers in calling for support in the fight against climate-change rules. "We've got precious few allies on this one."

"He's a stealth lobbyist," says John Passquentando, director of Ozone Action, a public interest research group. "Pearlman engages in deep lobbying, behind the scenes, influencing decision-makers when there is no one else around. Back in July [1997, Rep.] Tim Wirth (ID) said we need a legally-binding agreement to control greenhouse gases. But by December, the U.S. position had been radically altered in favor of the oil industry. This was in response to Pearlman's work."

PETER KNIGHT, behind-the-scenes and low-profile, is a real comer among Washington lobbyists because of his long history (since 1977) of close ties and role as chief fundraiser to Vice President Al Gore. As a lobbyist, he represents 14 companies, from Browning Ferris Industries to Walt Disney, and two regional

Bell systems, along with Lockheed Martin. In 1997 one of his clients won a $5 billion contract to clean up the Hanford nuclear weapons site in Washington.

In 1996 after more than a century of being ignored by Washington, the Cheyenne-Arapahoe, who had wanted to regain control of 10 acres in Oklahoma, decided to buy some attention by contributing $107,000 from an emergency fund to the Clinton-Gore re-election campaign. The contribution netted them a meeting with Clinton, and following a

> **A Real Comer Among Lobbyists Because of Connections to Al Gore**

contribution to his birthday party bash, they secured a dinner with Gore. Still nothing happened, so the Indians contacted Gore fundraiser Nathan Landow, who wanted to bring in Peter Knight. According to the *Washington Post*, "Landow touted access he and Knight have to top Clinton administration aides, and even explicitly warned he would ensure the tribes would not get their land back if they did not sign a development contract giving him 10 percent of the land's potentially lucrative mineral rights." Landow later denied the threat and Knight claimed he was only peripherally involved.

In the spring of 1995 Knight was looking for money when he approached one of his clients, Molten Metal Technology, Inc., a Massachusetts hazardous waste disposal firm, to raise $50,000 for the Clinton-Gore campaign. Afterwards, Gore visited the company's plant to mark Earth Day.

JAMES MCCLURE. For 20 years, Idaho's Senator James McClure stood as the arch-nemesis of environmentalists on Capitol Hill. As chairman of the Senate Committee on Energy and Natural Resources, McClure zealously guarded the interests of the mining and timber companies doing business on public lands. He

> **"In Idaho we don't have spotted owls. We shoot them at the border."**

is credited with single-handedly squashing repeated attempts to reform the archaic 1872 Mining Law and for stalling the designation of millions of acres of public land in Idaho and Montana as wilderness. He also used his clout to pass exemptions to the Endangered Species Act and other environmental laws that allowed timber and mining companies to continue to operate on lands occupied by endangered species, such as grizzly bears. McClure gained notoriety for his quip, "In Idaho we don't have spotted owls. We shoot them at the border."

After retiring from the Senate in 1990, McClure opened a firm specializing in mining issues and quickly amassed more than 30 clients.

One of McClure's first clients (and on whose board he sits) was the Idaho-based Boise Cascade, one of the largest purchasers of timber from the national forests. McClure maintains an even more profitable relationship with Coeur d'Alene Mining, which operates gold and silver mines on federal lands in Alaska, Idaho, California, and Nevada. As a director of the company McClure receives $50,000 a year. In addition, his lobbying firm was paid more than $150,000 to oppose efforts to reform the 1872 mining law, and to secure federal permits for the company's planned gold mine near Juneau, Alaska.

CECIL ANDRUS. Former Secretary of Interior under Jimmy Carter, Andrus joined the board of Coeur d'Alene soon after he stepped down as governor of Idaho, where he had faithfully served the interests of the mining companies for eight years. In 1993 Andrus led an upris-

> Former Idaho Governor, Now Mining Industry Lobbyist

ing of western Democrats against the Clinton administration's plans to begin charging royalties for gold and other minerals mined from federal lands. A week after Andrus's public remonstrance, the Clinton administration dropped the proposal from its budget request.

In early 1994, Andrus also took credit for engineering the ouster of Jim Baca as director of the Bureau of Land Management. Baca's efforts to impose more stringent environmental standards on livestock grazing and mining practices on the 250 million acres of public land in the West managed by the BLM had sparked a firestorm of protest from ranchers and mining companies in states such as New Mexico, Nevada, and Idaho. Andrus had called on Clinton and Interior Seretary Bruce Babbitt to sack Baca for being "out of control." In January 1994 Babbitt caved in to the pressure and removed Baca from his position.

Environmental Groups

EW ISSUES EXCITE THE PASSIONS of Americans more than environmental causes. Since the first Earth Day, the U.S. has witnessed a proliferation of green groups. One estimate by the IRS suggests that their may be as many as 12,000 groups working on environmental issues, ranging from small neighborhood associations to mammoth groups such as The Nature Conservancy that are difficult to distinguish from a downsized transnational corporation. Oregon alone counts more than 250 environmental groups, the most per capita in the nation.

Americans pour $3 billion into environmental groups every year. A sizable chunk of that money goes to the 12 largest organizations that dominate the green scene in Washington, DC. (Eight of the 12 are profiled below.) But most members have little idea where their money goes, how it is spent and whether the groups they support actually accomplish much. Most people simply join the group that sends them the most seductive direct mail solicitation, the insidious calling card of the big

> Groups such as The Nature Conservancy are difficult to distinguish from a downsized transnational corporation.

greens. The average supporter of these groups is generally unaware that often as much as 40 percent of their contribution will simply be recycled back into more fundraising, that another portion will go toward the six-figure salary of the group's CEO, or that their money might commingle with contributions from toxic corporations. One basic rule of thumb is that any group which can afford to send you a lot of glossy direct mail requests a year, probably doesn't need your money.

With all this money

GREENPEACE
Help end nuclear testing while we still have a chance.

rolling into the environmental movement, why has so little progress been made on cleaning up the nation's hazardous waste sites or stemming the destruction of our ancient forests?

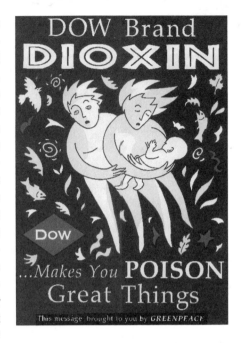

DOW Brand **DIOXIN**
...*Makes You* **POISON** Great Things
DOW
This message brought to you by *GREENPEACE*

Some critics, such as investigative journalist Mark Dowie, suggests that size does matter, in reverse:

> With all this money rolling into to the environmental movement, why has so little progress been made?

the larger a group gets, the more bureaucratic and less effective it becomes. As Dowie and others have noted, there is amazing work being done at the grassroots level against tremendous odds, but these struggles are often neglected by the press and unnoticed by the larger public.

The Mainstreams

Created in 1967 by a small band of lawyers seeking to ban DDT • evolved into George Bush's favorite environmental group • drafted blueprint for 1990 Clean Air revisions and endorsed Bush's "no net loss" of wetlands scheme • premier advocate of market-oriented solutions to environmental problems • excited about pollution credits, emissions trading systems, mitigation banking and user fees for recreational use of public lands • cheerleader for NAFTA • hosts the Barbra Streisand Chair of Environmental Studies, the perch of scientist Michael Oppenheimer, who advocates buying up development rights in the Third World as a solution to global climate change • convinced McDonald's to reform its solid waste disposal practices and to move from styrofoam to paper packaging • developed "paper use task force" in cooperation with major timber companies, and its recommendations discreetly ignored sustainable alternatives to paper, such as industrial hemp and kenaf • President Fred Krupp praised by *Inc.* magazine for his ability to "speak capitalism."

BUDGET	$18 MILLION
STAFF	120
MEMBERS	250,000
CEO SALARY	>$230,000
	INCLUDING BENEFITS

Sprang up out of protests against U.S. nuclear testing in the Aleutians • gained reputation as media-savvy, confrontational group with a radical eco-agenda to end pollution, protect biodiversity and bring about global disarmament • waged war against factory trawlers, whaling ships, pulp mills, and the French nuclear navy • saw membership explode to five million in 1990 (following the sinking of the Rainbow Warrior) • one of few national groups to demonstrate some sensitivity to the social and economic problems of Third World nations • valiantly fought NAFTA and GATT, but recently joined forces with NAFTA proponents in support of a controversial bill to

BUDGET	$20 MILLION
STAFF	250
MEMBERS	4 MILLION
CEO SALARY	>$65,000

weaken U.S. dolphin protection laws; smothered efforts to unionize its legions of canvassers • criticized in 1997 by 16 founding members for becoming too bureaucratic, lacking focus, and doling out high salaries • called the "Avon ladies of environmental movement" by ex-Greenpeacer, Cpt. Paul Watson of Sea Shepherd Society • August 1997, slashed its budget from $32 million to $20 million, closed its regional offices, and shut down its national canvass.

One of the oldest and most highbrow of American conservation groups • long a bastion of Rockefeller Republicans • demonstrates a particular obsession with Third World birth rates and has advocated harsh population control measures • in 1991 fired award-winning editor of *Audubon* magazine Les Line, replaced him with Malcolm Abrams, former editor of *The Star* tabloid • takes in hundreds of thousands of dollars from conservative foundations, such as Pew Charitable Trusts (Sun Oil), JM Kaplan Fund (a former pass-through for CIA monies) and Ford Foundation • purged staff in 1996, including Brock Evans, widely regarded as the best eco-lobbyist on the Hill • suppressed story in *Audubon* magazine by Pulitzer prize-winning writer Tom Wicker, because it was critical of Clinton; former staffers say new president, John Flicker, wants to turn it into a Nature Conservancy for the bird-watching crowd • has raked in millions from royalties on oil and gas wells in its Rainey Wildlife Reserve in Louisiana • local chapters, such as Sassafras Audubon in Bloomington, Indiana and Kalmiopsis Audubon

BUDGET	$40 MILLION
STAFF	300
MEMBERS	540,000
CEO SALARY	>$180,000
	INCLUDING BENEFITS

in Port Orford, Oregon, often demonstrate a refreshing degree of independence.

The National Wildlife Federation is the largest environmental group on planet with four million members • represents the old guard of the conservation establishment, including many hunting, fishing and gun clubs stained by a history of racism • for decades largely funded through sale of wildlife stamps • through 1980s and early 1990s the Federation was dominated by the personality and profligate habits of its CEO Jay Hair, who had a passion for limousines, expensive travel budgets, swank office furnishings and political deal-making; founded "Environmental Coalition for NAFTA" • opened its board of directors to corporate chieftains, including Dean Buntrock of Waste Management; favorite charity of John Denver and big oil companies, including Arco, Chevron and Mobil • Hair ousted in 1995, moved to Seattle, began flacking for timber company • faced with a funding crunch, new management of NWF scaled back operations, selling off group's lavish corporate headquarters in DC • new president Mark Van Putten expressed reservations about NAFTA expansion in Latin America, unclear whether group will fight inclusion of Chile with

BUDGET	$80 MILLION
STAFF	600
MEMBERS	4 MILLION
CEO SALARY	>$180,000
	INCLUDING BENEFITS

the same vigor they showed in huckstering the original trade pact.

The Natural Resources Defense Council was born in the wake of the first Earth Day, its bank accounts lavishly seeded by Rockefeller and Ford Foundation grants • early years spent litigating new litany of environmental laws, such as Clean Air Act and National Environmental Policy Act • by the 1980s had largely settled into an eco-think tank and lobby shop, generating monthly blizzards of white papers • stung (though vindicated) by Alar affair, now cautious about direct confrontations with corporations • betrayed Huaorani Indians in Ecuador by trying to broker a deal allowing oil development of tribal lands • favorite roost of Hollywood celebs, such as Robert Redford and Meryl Streep • zealous promoter of electric utility deregulation • founding member John Bryson, now heads nuke-laden Southern California Edison • unlikely to live down boast by executive director John Adams that NRDC had "broken the back

BUDGET	$25 MILLION
STAFF	130
MEMBERS	175,000
CEO SALARY	>$200,000
	INCLUDING BENEFITS

of the environmental opposition to NAFTA."

The titan of green groups; sits on nearly a billion dollars in assets; awash in cash, much of it coming from a tidal wave of corporate donations, including notorious polluters such as Arco, Archer-Daniels-Midland, British Petroleum, DuPont, Shell and Freeport McMoRan; eschews political work in favor of relatively non-controversial project of buying land; refers to itself as "Nature's real estate agent"; purchases private land then sells it to state and federal agencies, often, according to its critics, at a considerable mark-up; violated apolitical policy last year to concoct compromise rewrite of Endangered Species Act with a secret coalition of corporations and trade associations, including National Homebuilders and timber giant Georgia-Pacific; supported NAFTA; led by John Sawhill, former energy aide to Nixon and Ford, a fanatical proponent of nuclear power, who has enjoyed lucrative positions on boards of Procter & Gamble, North American Coal Company and Pacific Gas & Electric.

BUDGET	$337 MILLION
STAFF	1200
MEMBERS	720,000 INDIVIDUALS
	220 CORPORATIONS
CEO SALARY	>$200,000
	INCLUDING BENEFITS

Founded by John Muir, who preached a preservationist message that led to creation of Yosemite National Park • promotes itself as the nation's "oldest and most effective grassroots environmental organization" • largely settled into little more than a hiking club for the well-heeled from the Bay Area, until David Brower took the helm in the 1950s and led the group in great battles to save Grand Canyon, create Redwood National Park, and protect Alaskan wilderness • Brower ousted in 1969 after the Club lost tax-exempt status due to his aggressive political work • led in the 1980s by Douglas Wheeler, a Republican who now serves in California governor Pete Wilson's administration • fought hard against NAFTA and was an early proponent of environmental justice issues • still maintains the most democratic structure of any major group, though critics, such as Margaret Young, claim the Club leadership has used repressive measures to stifle dissent • under leadership of Carl Pope, an intimate of Al Gore, Club twice endorsed Clinton-Gore ticket over raucous objections of many members • 1996 ballot initiative calling for end to commercial logging on public lands overwhelmingly passed by Club membership, despite fierce opposition from the group's leaders and lobbyists • currently riding media hype of Gen-X board

BUDGET	$50 MILLION
STAFF	150
MEMBERS	550,000
CEO SALARY	>$100,000
	INCLUDING BENEFITS

president Adam Warbach • true leader to watch, Chad Hanson, who led the Zero Cut campaign to end logging on public lands to victory over opposition of Club leadership.

World Wildlife Fund was founded after World War II, its multi-tentacled international operations are now overseen by Prince Philip • promotes debt-for-nature swaps in the Third World; advocates hunting of rare wildlife species and lifting of worldwide ban on ivory trade • slavishly supports NAFTA and other international trade pacts • has pocketed contributions from timber, chemical, oil, and tobacco firms • board dominated by corporate chieftains • president is Roger Sant, CEO of AES power company, who prefers doing business in China because of Li Peng's fierce opposition to global environmental treaties • made millions off of panda logo products, but conservation efforts in China largely fizzled • cozy with Third World dictatorships • urged Canada to bestow a conservation award on Shell Oil, the company which provided arms to Nigerian "kill-and-go"

BUDGET	$65 MILLION
STAFF	250
MEMBERS	1 MILLION
CEO SALARY	>$200,000
	INCLUDING BENEFITS

police squads and stood silent as Ken Saro-Wiwa and seven other Ogoni organizers were marshaled to the gallows.

The New Environmental Movement

In recent years the environmental movement seems to have gone back to its roots. In part as a reaction to the perceived ineffectiveness of the large, DC-based organizations, the 1990s have seen a proliferation of small, locally-based environmental groups, which now number in the thousands, range from the Missoula, Montana-based Alliance for the Wild Rockies, which runs an astute international campaign to save wildlands and wildlife in the northern Rockies, to ad hoc community groups in places such as East Chicago, Indiana, which are united in efforts to fend off chemical dumps in their neighborhoods.

In general these grassroot groups have adopted a more populist and uncompromising posture than the DC-centered groups. They tend to focus more on the behavior of corporations than government regulators and have advanced progressive concepts of environmental and economic justice. Their tactics and strategies are also more aggressive, favoring litigation, media savvy direct action, and nonviolent civil disobedience over lobbying, white papers, and negotiation. The heroes of this new generation of activists are not the lobbyists and policy wonks who dominated the environmental scene in the 1970s and 1980s, but hardcore activists and visionaries, such as the late Edward Abbey, the toxic waste organizer Lois Gibbs, and David Brower. What follows is a sampling of some of best organizations in this new and vibrant environmental movement.

Alliance for the Wild Rockies

Shocked the West in 1990 with its outlandish proposal to preserve 16 million acres of land in Montana and Idaho as new national parks and wilderness areas; the best friend of the grizzly and bull trout; relentless, fierce and uncompromising; by far the most visionary group working on public lands issues.

> Alliance for the Wild Rockies
> PO Box 8731
> Missoula, MT 59807
> 406-721-5420

Chester Residents Concerned for Quality Living

Impoverished Pennsylvania community of Chester became a mecca for hazardous waste; five incinerators— marketed as resource recovery facilities—now loom over the town, spewing poison into the sky; unpaid CRCQL director Zulene Mayfield, operating on a budget of less than $15,000 a year, has led emotional protests against Westinghouse, despite death threats, break-ins, indifference of national greens and repeated acts of racist intimidation.

CRCQL
2731 West 3rd St.
Chester, PA 19013
610-485-0763

Earth First!

The radical environmental movement founded by Dave Foreman in the early 1980s, earned a reputation for confrontational activism, media-savvy protests, and monkey-wrenching. Earth First!ers tended to view themselves as western anarchists, in the tradition of Edward Abbey; brought a sense of humor and adventure to an often stuffy movement; they were also effective; led the fight to protect old-growth forests in the Pacific Northwest, challenged the destruction of the redwoods and were one of the first groups to speak passionately about protecting desert ecosystems; organization splintered apart in the early 1990s over internal conflicts about tree spiking, attitudes toward immigration, complaints over sexism and left-wing politics; Foreman left in a huff to publish the *Wild Earth* magazine; now it seems to represent more of an attitude than an identifiable group, but the *Earth First! Journal* remains one the best and most cantankerous environmental newspapers around.

Earth First! Journal
PO Box 1415
Eugene, OR 97440
541-741-9191

Earth Island Institute

Founded by eco-legend David Brower in 1982, after his radicalism caused him to be booted from first the Sierra Club, then Friends of the Earth; probably most visionary and creative American green group; tackles wide array of issues, from sea turtle protection to helping indigenous people in Borneo fend off timber companies; innovative Urban Habitat project, directed by Carl Anthony, advocates redesign of cities to make them safer and more livable landscapes; executive director Dave Phillips has led fight to preserve U.S. dolphin protection laws, taking on the likes of the U.S. State Department, Don Young, Mexican drug cartels, Al

Earth Island Institute
300 Broadway St. Suite 28
San Francisco, CA 94133
415-788-3666

Gore, and Greenpeace; *Earth Island Journal* is the liveliest and most comprehensive magazine covering the environment.

Food & Water The small Vermont group that awakened America to the dangers of BGH, the dairy cow hormone; attacked plans to irradiate fruits and vegetables; exposed the dangerous levels of residual pesticides in lettuce; issued a ground-breaking report on economic concentration in the meat industry; executive director Mike Colby, the food industry's most feared and hated critic, eschews Beltway deal-making as "activist malpractice"; Colby now finds himself the target of food disparagement lawsuits; and shows no sign of backing down.

> Food & Water
> RR 1 Box 68D
> Walden, VT 05873
> 802-563-3300

Hoosier Environmental Council One of the first of the state environmental councils and still one of the best; in the past 12 years HEC has battled steel mills, hazardous waste firms, coal companies, utilities, chemical agriculture and the U.S. Forest Service and usually won; working on environmental justice issues in Gary long before such matters became trendy and long after the funding community moved on to other priorities.

> Hoosier Environmental Council
> 1002 E. Washington St., Ste. 300
> Indianapolis, IN 46202
> 317-685-8800

International Rivers Network From its frugal offices in Berkeley, IRN has tirelessly battled the World Bank, transnational corporations and the National Security Council in an effort to fight dams across the globe; has caused more problems for the Chinese leaders than Jesse Helms and John Huang combined; probably generates more bang for the buck than any other American environmental group.

> International Rivers Network
> 1847 Berkeley Way
> Berkeley, CA 94703
> 510-848-1155

Native Forest Council Perhaps the distinguishing attribute of the Native Forest Council was its early realization that biological systems could not survive endless rounds of political compromise. America's heritage forests, shorn and fragmented in the past century, were a clearcut testament that compromise as an instrument of forest management policy meant only one thing: more logging; was the first to advocate no logging at all on

Native Forest Council
P.O. Box 2190
Eugene, OR 97402
541-688-2600

public lands, rather than argue over the rate of forest destruction. Zero Cut.

Project Underground

A new group located adjacent to IRN in Berkeley that has already more than filled the void left by mainstream groups working on mining and oil extraction in the developing world; defines its mission as the protection of human rights threatened by mining and oil companies; while the World Wildlife Fund was clamoring for an award for Shell, Project Underground was busy exposing the oil giant's ties to Nigerian death squads; now targeting Freeport McMoRan's toxic mining operation in

Project Underground
1847 Berkeley Way
Berkeley, CA 94703
510-705-8981

Indonesia that has decimated the Amungme people.

Rachel's Environment and Health Weekly

Not a group, per se, but an influential newsletter produced by Peter Montague of the Environmental Research Foundation; provides cutting edge analysis in clear prose of complex science on toxics, corporate accountability and progressive green politics; unafraid to challenge tactics of mainstream enviros; in a word: indispensable.

Rachel's Environment
and Health Weekly
PO Box 5036
Annapolis, MD 21403
410-263-1584

Save America's Forests

Started on a shoestring budget in the early 1990s, premised on the notion that grassroots forest activists needed a presence on Capitol Hill. Carl Ross and Mark Winstein found a cheap office near the Library of Congress, and rapidly began one of the most influential environmental outfits in Washington; has effectively fended off dozens of bad bills with their unique brand of on-the-spot activism; have also promoted a positive agenda, crafting legislation that would dramatically overhaul forest management on public lands by ending the practice of clearcutting and by requiring all old-growth forests and roadless areas to be set

Save America's Forests
4 Library Court, SE
Washington, DC 20003
202-544-9229

aside from loggers' chainsaws: the Act to Save America's Forest, has been endorsed by 600 scientists, including E.O. Wilson and Jane Goodall.

Snake River Alliance

This Boise-based group has taken on nuclear weapons production and radioactive waste storage at the Idaho National Engineering Lab; program director Beatrice Brailsford made former Energy Secretary Hazel O'Leary's enemies list, right behind Bob Dole as DOE's most trenchant critic; so effective that a top secret Idaho National Guard security assessment labeled this pacifist group a potential "opposing force."

Snake River Alliance
Box 1731
Boise, ID 83701
208-344-9161

Southwest Network for Environmental and Economic Justice

The nation's premier environmental justice outfit; a five-year-old coalition of 80 groups from eight states in the American Southwest, at least three Mexican states, and several Indian reservations; led by Richard Moore, a longtime activist for Latino rights, who is battling a Strategic Litigation Against Public Participation suit brought by NuMex; now fighting the migration of hi-tech companies to the Southwest, pointing out that most of the horrific environmental and economic costs of these industries are borne by poor communities and people of color.

SNEEJ
PO Box 7399
Albuquerque, NM 87192
505-242-0416

Western Organization of Resource Councils

Organizes small farmers and ranchers in West against import of toxic waste; promotes reforms of archaic and destructive mining laws; challenges monopolization of meat packing industry; fights for family farms; develops organizing skills for grassroots leaders.

WORC
2401 Montana Ave #301
Billings, MT 59101
406-252-9672

David R. Brower

Environmentalist, Founder and President of Earth Island Institute

AGE:
86

NICKNAME:
The
Archdruid

EDUCATION:
Attended the
University of
California at
Berkeley;
claims to have
graduated
from the
University of
the Colorado
River

GREATEST ACHIEVEMENT:
Keeping the Bureau of Reclamation from building a
dam in Grand Canyon through a relentless lobbying
campaign and an innovative public relations campaign,
typified by a full-page ad in the New York Times which
asked: "Should We Flood the Sistine Chapel
So Tourists Can Get Nearer the Ceiling?"

GREATEST DISAPPOINTMENT:
Failing to stop the construction of the dam that buried
Glen Canyon under water and silt. Brower made a deal
during the Eisenhower administration that allowed the
dam at Glen Canyon to go up in exchange for keeping a
dam out of Dinosaur National Monument on the Green
River. Brower has spent much of the last 30 years trying
to bring down Glen Canyon dam. "Never trade a place
you know for one you don't," Brower cautions.

QUOTE:
"We don't inherit the earth,
we borrow it from our grandchildren."

Background on David Brower

When David Brower became executive director of the Sierra Club in the early 1950s, the Sierra Club was little more than a small social group for rich white males from the San Francisco Bay Area who liked to climb mountains. Brower quickly transformed

> Brower's confrontational style quickly earned him a lot of political enemies.

the Club into the nation's most powerful environmental group waging great battles to save the Grand Canyon, create new national parks, and protect the great Alaskan wilderness. Brower's confrontational style quickly earned him a lot of political enemies, including some old-guard members of the Club. His successful campaign to stop the dam planned for Grand Canyon ultimately prompted the IRS to yank the Club's treasured status as a tax-deductible charity. Brower also took the Club into new issues, such as pollution, pesticides, worker safety, and matters of environmental justice.

Brower was an early opponent of nuclear power, an issue that cost him his job. Several Sierra Club board members, including photographer Ansel Adams, had cut a deal with Pacific Gas & Electric to change the site of the utility's new nuclear plant from Nipomo Dunes to Diablo Canyon. Brower publicly attacked the Diablo Canyon site, noting that its location on a major faultline was a recipe for disaster. This impertinence led to Brower's ouster from the Club in 1969. He didn't stop. Brower went on to found Friends of the Earth, an international environmental group known for taking on corporations and the global military establishment, and Earth Island Institute, which has challenged international trade agreements and led the campaign to protect whales, sea turtles and dolphins. Brower has twice been nominated for the Nobel Peace Prize and remains the world's most visionary and radical environmentalist.

Glen Canyon Dam

On September 13, 1963, the last bucket of concrete was poured into Glen Canyon Dam, completing what was to become perhaps the most reviled construction project in American history. Behind the 700-foot tall arc of concrete, the Colorado River flowed for more than two years to fill the 186-mile long reservoir called Lake Powell, after John Wesley Powell, the one-armed Civil War veteran who was the first man to float down the Colorado.

Glen Canyon Dam never was meant to provide water to the parched cities of the Southwest. Only the small town of Page, Arizona, population 8,000, draws its drinking water from Lake Powell. Instead, this $270 million structure was built as a kind of holding pond, to slow the flow of the Colorado and keep the water from, as one Bureau of Reclamation watercrat put it, "being wasted on Mexico."

The dam was built to keep the water from "being wasted on Mexico."

But the massive reservoir itself is tremendously wasteful. Every year nearly a million-acre-feet of water disappears from Lake Powell. Some of it is lost through evaporation under the searing desert sun. But most of the water is being extracted by the canyon itself; its porous sandstone walls absorb massive amounts of water through a phenomenon known as bank storage. One million-acre-feet is a staggering amount of water, equal to more than 8 percent of the Colorado's annual flow and enough water to serve Denver for more than four years.

Another unforeseen problem is silt. It's piling up much faster than predicted. In fact, in 200 years the sediment flushed down the Colorado will have topped the dam, leaving it as a 700-foot tall manmade waterfall. Silt's also a problem downstream, on the free-flowing stretch of the Colorado as it winds through the Grand Canyon. But here the problem is a lack of silt. As a result, sandbars along the river are disappearing, seriously degrading the riparian habitat that is so important to the wildlife of Grand Canyon National Park.

The Glen Canyon Dam contains a large hydroturbine that was supposed to generate 1300 megawatts of electricity. But operating at this capacity proved to be so harmful to downstream conditions that it was scaled back to about 650 megawatts a year. Since the dam went on-line there has been a power surplus in the Four Corners states. As a result most of Glen Canyon's power is sold to industrial users at heavily subsidized rates.

Glen Canyon Dam's biggest backer was Floyd Dominy, the head of the Bureau of Reclamation. Dominy said that the dam would create "a blue jewel in the desert" that would prove a tourist mecca for this remote area. Indeed, more than a million people a year visit 190,000-acre Lake Powell, cruising across its flat surface on jet skis and houseboats. But more people each year visit the undammed segments of the Colorado at Grand Canyon and Canyonlands. And since the dam went up, whitewater rafting has become one of the most popular and lucrative recreational sports in the

> The dam has come to symbolize the awful cost of political deal-making and compromise.

West. Hundreds of Anazazi ruins and petroglyphs were inundated and more than a dozen endangered species lost, as well as hundreds of miles of canyons that have been described as among the most beautiful on Earth.

More than any other issue, Glen Canyon Dam sparked the birth of a new environmental movement: grassroots-based, militant, and deeply suspicious of the federal bureaucracy. To the writer Edward Abbey, Glen Canyon Dam was an assault on the essential value of the American spirit of freedom, the freedom of a wild flowing river. To David Brower, the dam came to symbolize the awful cost of political deal-making and compromise. In 1956, Brower had traded off Glen Canyon, a place he'd never seen, for a deal to keep a dam from being built on the Green River in Dinosaur National Park. Even the archconservative Barry Goldwater looked at Glen Canyon Dam with regret. He said on his retirement that if he could recast one vote in his long Senate career, it would be the vote to build Glen Canyon Dam.

Now 35 years after its construction, there has been a call to drain Lake Powell, tear down the dam, and let the Colorado flow free again. It is to that invigorating prospect that we dedicate our book.

Resources

FEC Info. This independent web page provides an online database of all contributions to federal candidates, political action committees, and "soft money" contributions to political parties: www.tray.com/fecinfo.

Center For Responsive Politics. An excellent source for discovering how lobbyists wield their power in Washington for their corporate clients. The CRP website maintains a list of all federal lobbyists, their clients, the issues they work on, and their fees. In addition, the Center issues excellent reports on trade associations and how PACs used their political contributions and lobbying might to influence legislation. The Center for Responsive Politics, 1320 19th Street NW, Suite 620, Washington, DC 20036 (202) 857-0044, www.crp.org.

Security Exchange Commission Edgar Database. The place to look for detailed information on publicly-traded corporations. The SEC's Edgar system houses all the required corporate filings, including proxy statements, prospectuses, and quarterly and annual reports. Most corporations will also send you these documents on request: www.edgar-online.com.

Environmental Protection Agency. The EPA is a rich trove of information. Particularly valuable is the agency's biannual publication called, *Toxic Release Inventory*. The TRI report lists the top air, water, and land toxic polluters by region and by the toxic chemicals they produce. The TRI is available online (www.epa.gov/enviro/html/tris) and from the EPA a three-volume set by calling 202-260-1545. The EPA also provides a daily clipping service summarizing news stories across the country on environmental matters. The report is free and is delivered via email. To subscribe, send the command subscribe OPPT-NEWSBREAK Firstname Lastname to listserver @valley.rtpnc.epa.gov.

Rachel's Environment and Health Weekly. Quite simply the best environmental newsletter in America with detailed and informative reporting on toxic waste, chemical pollution, environmental politics, and environmental justice issues. For information write: PO Box 5036, Annapolis, MD 21403.

Index